FELICIA CARTRIGHT
AND THE
LONE SKI BOOT

Felicia   Joan

FELICIA CARTRIGHT

AND THE
LONE SKI BOOT

BERNARD PALMER

ANEKO
PRESS

Aneko Press Youth

www.anekopress.com

Aneko Press, Life Sentence Publishing, and our logos are trademarks of
Life Sentence Publishing, Inc.
203 E. Birch Street
P.O. Box 652
Abbotsford, WI 54405

JUVENILE FICTION / Religious / Christian / Action & Adventure

Paperback ISBN: 979-8-88936-314-9

eBook ISBN: 979-8-88936-315-6

10   9   8   7   6   5   4   3   2   1

Available where books are sold

CONTENTS

CHAPTER 1

A LOCKED DOOR

Joan Bailey stormed up the worn stairs and swept angrily along the narrow corridor of the dormitory at Wellington School for Girls to the room she shared with Felicia Cartright. Her proper "Wellington" shoes clicked a stuttering vibrato on the terrazzo floor, and her fingers clutched the English textbook so tightly her knuckles showed white. Her eyes blazed, and twin spots of fire glowed in her ashen cheeks. Miss Duncan would have chided her severely for it had she seen her then.

"Anger is unbecoming to a proper Wellington girl," she would have pointed out curtly.

But at the moment, Joan would not have paid any attention to the stern, unbending dean of women. Miss Duncan had been the cause of her irritation in the first place.

"Hi, Joan," a girl from across the hall sang out as the popular young brunette hurried by.

Joan only mumbled without slackening her pace.

"Can you come in for a moment? I've got something to show you."

"Can't right now. I've got to study."

"You study?" Her friend laughed pleasantly. "That's a switch."

"Well, don't die laughing over it!"

The hurt on the other girl's face plunged a dart into Joan. She shouldn't have said what she did. It wasn't Millie's fault that Miss Duncan had been so unreasonable.

Joan would have gone back to tell her she was sorry, but Millie was out of sight and her door was shut. When Joan entered her room, Felicia was sprawled on the bed reading a history assignment.

"Hi, Joan." There was surprise in her roommate's voice. "I didn't expect to see you back quite so soon."

"What Miss Duncan had to say to me didn't take long." Joan flounced over to the desk and threw her book on it. "I don't know what's gotten into her lately. The harder I work, the more she expects of me!"

"I always thought she was fair with everyone."

"That's because you're a pet of hers." Joan snorted. "Do you know how much extra time she gave me to get that horrible English theme finished? She gave me forty-eight hours! Imagine! That's only two days. Practically no time at all."

Felicia closed the book she had been reading and, with a toss of her blond head, swung her feet over the side of the bed and sat up.

"I hate to remind you of this, Joan," she said in a tone that revealed she didn't really mind it too much, "but I have been after you for the last two weeks to get your theme finished. You've known all along that they were supposed to be handed in by Friday."

"There you go," Joan retorted without anger, "sounding like Miss Duncan again. It isn't enough that I have to suffer under an uncompromising tyrant at school. I have to room with one too."

"I feel sorry for you," Felicia said, laughing.

"You don't need to," Joan said. "I'm doing a good job of feeling sorry for myself."

"It would help a lot more if you'd get to studying instead."

Joan got to her feet and crossed the room to the window. For a time, all was silent as she stared at the bleak, lifeless scene. The leaves had long since fallen from the trees and had been raked and carried off to be burned. Snow had covered snow until the lawn was a sea of white, and the sidewalks were piled high on either side with snow scooped from the narrow strip of cement between them. Joan watched a sparrow flutter down and perch on the sill just outside the window. The bird's head cocked curiously, as though he felt some kinship with the girl inside. She had the same feeling.

"That sparrow is just like I am," she murmured. "He doesn't have any more sense than to stick around where he's not wanted either." She pulled in a deep breath. "I'm not going to put up with Miss Duncan and all the rules here at Wellington anymore. I'm going to write Dad tonight and tell him that I want to go to some other school."

Felicia listened without concern to her friend's threat to leave Wellington. There had been a time after Joan first appeared on campus when nobody ever thought she would stay or that the school authorities would want to keep her, but it was different now. For all of Joan's talk about leaving, Felicia knew that it would break her roommate's heart to go somewhere else.

"Miss Duncan will have to get somebody else to pick on," Felicia giggled.

Joan spun on her heel to face her. "You think I won't, don't you? That's what Miss Duncan thinks too! She's got the idea that I'm married to this school or something and that she can say anything she wants to me and I'll stay here and take it. Well, I'll show her. I'll show all of you! I don't have to stay at Wellington. I'm going to some other school where I'll be appreciated."

"It's not as bad as all that." Felicia pushed her hair into place with long, slender fingers. "All you've got to do to get along here is study enough to get your grades up."

Joan made a face at Felicia. She knew she would lose the argument, but she wasn't going down without a battle. "You're just like Miss Duncan," she stormed. "You've got easy answers for everything!"

Felicia stood by the desk in front of her roommate.

"Instead of all this storming, you could be spending that energy on writing your theme, you know."

Joan sat down and opened her laptop. She banged furiously on the keyboard for two or three minutes like she was stepping on ants. Then she stopped with a suddenness that surprised Felicia.

"You know, I met Emma Valdez in the corridor again today," she exclaimed.

Felicia murmured something. They roomed next to Emma. It wasn't exactly surprising that they should meet her in the corridor. The past several days, however, Emma had not been acting normally. Now that Felicia thought about it, she realized that it had been almost a week since she had seen the new Cuban student in the lounge. Emma Valdez had been coming out of her room to go to classes and meals but that had been all anyone had seen of her lately. The rest of the time she spent locked in her room.

"Did you get to talk to her?" Felicia asked.

Joan shook her head, for the moment forgetting her own troubles. "She didn't act as though she wanted to talk with anybody, and she looked as though she had been crying or something."

Felicia toyed with her history book for a time. It

was disturbing to think that Emma was upset enough to cry. She hadn't seemed to be the kind who was given to tears. From the first day she appeared at Wellington, her charming smile and dark, flashing eyes had won the friendship of all who met her. She had a cheerfulness that couldn't be put down.

"You think I am say funny thing, no?" she would ask in class after getting her tongue hopelessly tangled in the jungle of English grammar. "But I am thinking this English is funny language."

"I figured maybe Miss Duncan has been trying to shape her into the model Wellington girl," Joan said. "That's enough to bring tears to anybody's eyes."

But Felicia did not agree. Miss Duncan was severe and uncompromising, even she would admit. But the dean of women wasn't cruel. It would be unthinkable that Miss Duncan would push a foreigner who was unused to American ways to the place of tears.

About all anyone at Wellington knew about Emma Valdez was that she was Cuban and had come to the rather unlikely place of an exclusive girl's school for her education. But there was an air of mystery about her, even from the first, and the entire school was aflame with speculation about this new girl who had such trouble with English.

It may have been Emma's simplicity that excited the imagination or the deceptively casual manner in which she came to Wellington. The day before orientation was to begin, she appeared at the school wearing an expensive dress and carrying a single suitcase of top grain cowhide. She neither tried to hide nor accentuate her Spanish accent. It was there, and anyone who associated with her would have to take it as well. But, for all of her simplicity, she carried herself with the easy grace of one born to wealth. Felicia had noticed that she had the same air of the other girls at Wellington whose parents were extremely rich.

But, on the one occasion when Felicia had seen Emma's closet, she had been surprised to find that it was almost bare. Felicia and Joan, whose wardrobes were far from large, had twice as many clothes. But it didn't seem to bother Emma that she had so few clothes or that the other girls knew about it. She was as merry and as unpredictable as the objects that decorated the walls in her room.

On one wall, she had a small Cuban flag with a motto in Spanish beneath it. Both Joan and Felicia would have liked to have a translation of it, but they didn't dare to ask. On the opposite side of the room, where another girl had hung the picture of a boyfriend, Emma displayed a single ski boot, only slightly used. This was something Felicia could not refrain from asking about.

"What on earth do you do with this?" she asked, pointing to the boot.

"What you do with a ski boot in America?" Emma asked, eyes laughing.

"You don't ski in Cuba," Joan reminded her.

"Just because we are Cuban doesn't mean we stay always in Cuba." Then the teasing died in her voice. "My mother used to go to Switzerland often when she was my age. The boot is my memory of her." A certain sadness crept in. "Now nobody from Cuba go anywhere to do anything."

But the sadness had been there for only a moment. Then the laughter came rushing back, and she was happy again. That was why it was so hard for the girls to think of Emma as being discouraged and unhappy.

* * *

Felicia and Joan went down to dinner together that evening. They looked for Emma along the way and were surprised to find her already in the hall waiting to get into the dining room.

"Hi," Felicia said brightly.

Emma's gaze met hers briefly. For an instant, her lips parted as though she was about to speak. Then she stiffened and turned away. In the dining hall, she took a seat at a table in a far corner where she was likely to be alone.

"She does act strange, doesn't she?" Felicia murmured.

"That's what I've been trying to tell you. She treated me the same way this afternoon."

"She acts as though she doesn't want to be around anyone she might have to talk to."

As soon as the attractive Cuban student finished eating, she got up from the table and hurried out. Passing Felicia and Joan, she kept her eyes averted to avoid having to speak to them.

"I can't figure it out," Felicia said. "She doesn't act like herself at all."

"You can say that again."

"She acts to me as though she's in some sort of trouble."

"Oh, no!" Joan groaned and rolled her eyes helplessly. "Not that!"

Felicia stuck out her tongue at her friend.

"Every time you get to talking that way, we wind up in a mess of trouble."

On the way back to their room, Felicia went over to Emma's door and knocked softly.

"Emma," she called, knocking again. "Emma!"

No answer.

"Maybe she's gone out somewhere."

Felicia tried the door quietly.

"No," she whispered. "She's inside. The door is locked."

Concern flickered in Joan's eyes. "What do you suppose is wrong?"

CHAPTER 2

EMMA'S ARRIVAL

Reluctantly, Felicia left Emma's locked dormitory door and followed Joan into their own room.

"I don't mind telling you, I'm concerned about Emma."

"She is acting strange," Joan replied, "I'll have to admit. But it might not be anything any more serious than a boyfriend who hasn't been writing as often as he promised."

That explanation didn't satisfy Felicia. "She doesn't seem to be the type."

The Cartright girl was in her pajamas before she spoke again. "Most of us get upset and discouraged once in a while. I wouldn't think anything about it if it was anyone else but Emma."

Her roommate's eyes narrowed. "What's so special about her?"

"You were here when she came in the first time, weren't you?" Felicia reminded her.

Her friend nodded. Who could forget an event like the arrival of Emma Valdez? Nobody had even known she was coming – at least among the girls – until a rental car pulled up at the front door and a slight, dark-skinned man got out and went around to the passenger's side to open the door. Joan Bailey had been the one who spotted them first. She was always the first one to notice handsome men on campus.

"Look, Felicia."

She was pointing at the olive-skinned man; but, when Felicia glanced through the lounge window, she first saw the new student. The girl getting out of the car was as dark as Felicia was fair. Her hair was raven-black and straight except for the gentle waves that arched gracefully over her ears. Her skin was as dark as that of a southern lifeguard at the end of summer, but it was smooth and flawless.

She moved gracefully, a poised, slender figure of loveliness who could easily be the envy of every girl in school – and probably would be, Felicia observed silently. But, with all of that, a joy of living seemed to sparkle in the newcomer's quick smile and large black eyes. She was talking as she approached the dormitory with her companion, her face reflecting the excitement of the moment.

Instinctively, Felicia felt that this was a girl who would be interesting to know.

The man was as handsome as the girl was beautiful, only in a different way. He was impeccably dressed and wore a thin wisp of a neatly groomed moustache. He, too, was dark, but older than the girl by a dozen years or more.

They stopped in front of the receptionist.

"Is Miss Duncan in?" he asked in flawless English.

The girl at the desk reached for the phone. "Who should I say is calling?"

"Hermano Valdez. She is expecting me."

Conversation in the lounge choked off as the girls eyed the newcomers curiously. They were not American. Felicia and Joan were sure of that. There was something indefinably foreign about the cut of their clothes and their manner. Hermano Valdez spoke English as perfectly as though he had first learned to lisp the language at his mother's knee. The girl spoke credibly enough. It was obvious that she had studied English for several years, but more than a trace of accent betrayed her Spanish ancestry.

Joan leaned over and whispered to her roommate, "Isn't she beautiful?"

Felicia nodded. Emma was, indeed, more beautiful than anyone else in the lounge. And yet she seemed to be completely unaware of it, as though it mattered not at all. And she carried herself with dignity. Felicia knew that Miss Duncan would heartily approve of her.

The dean of women was not long in coming out. The door to her office opened, and she appeared, eyes narrowed severely. "Mr. Valdez?" she asked.

"You must be Miss Duncan." He bowed slightly. "I've been expecting you. Won't you come in?"

"Thank you." He spoke simply enough but seemed to give the words a special inflection that added meaning to them. He stepped to one side to allow the girl to precede him.

When the trio disappeared behind the door, conversation in the lounge exploded into being once more. The girls were looking at one another questioningly.

"Who is she?"

"Where did she come from?"

"Is she going to school here?"

Joan Bailey shrugged. "I don't know the answers to any of those questions, but I can tell you this much. If I had a boyfriend, I wouldn't let him see her if I could help it. I'm afraid he would be long gone."

It was some time before Miss Duncan's office door opened and the trio reappeared.

"I shall leave Emma in your care, Miss Duncan," Hermano Valdez was saying.

"She will get along quite nicely with us, señor."

The faintest wisp of a smile lighted the man's bleak face. "That is something of which we are well aware. We learned as much before we ever contacted you."

He took the girl's hand and pressed it to his lips. Then he turned and hurried across the lounge and down the stone steps to his waiting car. He did not look back.

Miss Duncan remained motionless for a time,

surveying the girls in the lounge. Then, her smile flashing, she came over to where Felicia and Joan were sitting. "I would like to have you meet our new student, girls." Flashing her company smile and using her cultured company voice, she introduced them to Emma Valdez.

"I am so glad to know you," Emma replied.

Both Felicia and Joan felt that she truly meant it.

After introducing Emma to the other girls in the dormitory lounge, Miss Duncan brought her back to Felicia and Joan. "I have a hundred things to do this afternoon. I really must be going. Will you girls be kind enough to look after Emma for me?"

She put the statement in the form of a question, but both girls knew it was not a question, it was a command. She wanted them to show the newcomer around the school and introduce her to as many other girls as possible. It was their responsibility to see that Emma Valdez learned enough about the Wellington campus and student body to be thrilled at the prospect of going to school there. Miss Duncan would be checking back later to see how thoroughly they had discharged their responsibility.

"Do you want us to help you get your things up to your room before we show you around?" Joan asked.

Emma's smile was warm and infectious. "It will be no trouble for me to manage. I have only one suitcase."

Joan knew that surprise and prying were both

taboo as far as the proper Wellington girl was concerned, but she could not help it. One suitcase for the school year, when most girls moved in by the truckload, was enough to prompt questioning.

"You mean you've got all your clothes and things for the whole year in that one suitcase?" she asked.

"Sí." Emma made no other explanation.

Joan was more curious than ever.

They went up to the room Miss Duncan had assigned Emma.

"You're going to be right next to us," Felicia said. "How nice."

"Who is your roommate going to be?"

The newcomer pivoted to face Joan. "Uncle Hermano felt that it is better if I have room alone."

Joan put another question mark in her mental notebook as she pondered that statement. She was going to ask something more about his reason for it, but Felicia was already starting down the corridor, chattering away as she gave Emma a rundown on the girls on their floor.

They went through the dormitory, across the campus to the classroom buildings, and into the library. On the way, Felicia and Joan introduced her to all the girls they met. That was one reason Miss Duncan often gave them the task of showing the campus to new students. She knew they would make an effort to see that the new girls got acquainted with as many upper classmen as they had opportunity to meet.

Emma seemed to be enjoying the tour. Even when her face was serious, there was joy in her eyes.

"You speak English very well," Joan said as they sat in the dining room that evening.

"Thank you." Her smile came and went. "I study English for four years back home in Cuba. Only now, when I am finally here, I think I do not know English at all."

At the mention of the little island country just off the coast of Florida, conversation at the rest of their table stopped. The girls gazed at Emma with deeper interest.

"Did you say you are from Cuba?" Felicia asked.

"Sí." She volunteered no more information.

"How long has it been since you left home?" Joan asked.

"It was five–" the girl counted on her fingers. "Maybe six weeks ago. Yes, it is six weeks, I think."

"How did you come here, Emma?" Joan asked. "Did you come out by plane as a part of that arrangement the United States has with the Cuban government?"

The girl stiffened. It seemed to Felicia that the color faded from her cheeks and her lips narrowed to a thin, hard line.

"No," Emma retorted curtly. "I do not come out under the arrangement with the government."

Joan gasped. Miss Duncan would have been horrified, but Joan couldn't help it. "Then how did you get out?"

Emma's gaze rested on her calmly. There was no anger – no hint of embarrassment. "I am here. That is the important thing."

Felicia changed the subject quickly, but Joan could think of little else all evening. As soon as she and Felicia were in their room alone, she gave voice to the questions that had been plaguing her.

"What is it with Emma, anyway?" She spoke guardedly, so she would not be overheard.

"What do you mean?"

"There's something strange about her," Joan continued. "She comes to school wearing a dress that probably cost half as much as either your whole wardrobe or mine, but she has all of the rest of her clothes in one suitcase."

"Maybe there's more luggage coming later."

Joan drew herself up indignantly. "I suppose you're aware of the fact that you're ruining *my* mystery with explanations like that – if they're true."

"I'll have to admit," Felicia added, "that there are some strange things about Emma. The fact that her uncle insists on her rooming alone, for one thing."

"And the way she got out of Cuba for another. Did you see that look on her face when I asked her how she managed to leave?"

Felicia nodded. "I was as surprised as you were to find her evasive. I've heard some of the refugees who escaped from Cuba give speeches, but I've never come across one before who wouldn't tell how he got out of the country."

Joan thought about that for a moment. "The only logical reason I can think of for her to be so secretive is that the people who helped her get out are still there, and she might be getting them in trouble if she tells anything."

Felicia went over to the dressing table and sat down to put up her hair. "That's probably as good a reason as she could possibly have for keeping quiet, but it makes me all the more curious."

"You'd just as well put that curiosity of yours back in mothballs," Joan told her. "You're not going to get any information from Emma Valdez."

Felicia paused with the brush in her hand.

"You know, there is something awfully mysterious about her."

* * *

Everybody at Wellington School for Girls was curious about the stunning Cuban stranger who had come there to go to school. In the days that followed, they gathered bits and pieces of information about her. They learned that the man who had brought her to the school was her father's brother, Hermano Valdez. One of the girls in the business office with a glaring breach of Wellington etiquette let it slip that Hermano had made a down payment on her tuition and board and room and said he would be back to take care of the balance. That had been weeks before, and nobody had seen or heard of him since.

Two or three times, Miss Duncan asked Emma if she had heard from her uncle.

"Sí," she said, her face crinkling. "He say he will write, but he no do it. Now it is many days since I hear from my Uncle Hermano."

"You will let me know when he writes to you, won't you, Emma?"

Questions gleamed in the girl's black eyes, but she did not voice them. "Sí." She spoke quickly. "I will let you know, señora – I mean señorita."

Miss Duncan gave no indication that she had even heard the girl's slip of tongue.

The school authorities waited as long as they felt they could before talking with Emma about the balance of her bill. Then Miss Duncan brought up the subject carefully, so the girl would not become alarmed. Still, it had disturbed Emma, and she came to Joan and Felicia about it.

"I no understand," she said in that lilting, musical accent of hers, "I see Uncle Hermano give Miss Duncan some money. Now she say there is something more to pay."

"Maybe he didn't pay enough for the entire year," Joan offered in explanation.

"What they do to me? Do they make me leave?" Although Emma tried hard to hide it, there was fear in her voice.

"Oh, no," Felicia said with a confidence she hoped was justified. "I'm sure they'll be able to work out something. Besides, your uncle will be getting in touch with the school before long."

"Sí," Emma replied hopefully.

* * *

But the weeks had stretched on, and still no one heard from Uncle Hermano. Now there was this sudden change in Emma – this unfriendliness and the evidence of tears.

"It's not like her at all," Felicia observed, "to meet us in the hall without speaking or to have her eyes swollen as though she's been crying."

"It must have something to do with Uncle Hermano and the fact that he hasn't written," Joan said.

"Maybe Miss Duncan has had to tell her that she can't go to school anymore unless her bill is paid. I happen to know that money for scholarships hasn't been coming in the way they would like to have it."

Joan got to her feet uneasily, her partially completed English theme forgotten for the moment. "It would be terrible if Emma would have to leave Wellington when she wants to stay here so badly."

Felicia pulled in a deep breath. "Maybe that isn't what's troubling her at all."

"I wouldn't know about that," Joan continued, "but, whatever it is, it's serious or she wouldn't be so upset about it."

CHAPTER 3

ENCOUNTER IN THE PARKING LOT

Felicia tried to study, but the pages became a blur before her eyes and all she could see was the sad face of Emma Valdez. The Cuban girl was probably lying on the bed, sobbing out her loneliness and frustration.

Felicia knew just how she felt. She had felt the same way many times in the months before she became acquainted with the person of Jesus Christ and turned her life over to Him.

Felicia flinched visibly.

The thought stabbed into her consciousness. She didn't know why she had never realized it before; but, suddenly, she saw that in all the times she and Joan had talked with Emma, they had never once presented Christ to her. They had never talked with her about the claims He had on her life.

That could be the reason Emma was so disturbed. She was trying to carry all of her problems alone when she could look to Jesus for strength and help. Felicia didn't know whether Emma would have listened or not, but that wasn't any excuse. She had never given her the chance!

Felicia could stand it no longer. "I'll be back in a little while, Joan," she said, starting for the door.

"It won't do you any good," her roommate said without looking up. "Emma doesn't want to talk with anybody tonight."

"I've got to try," Felicia insisted, stepping out into the hall. She knocked guardedly on the door next to theirs, but Joan was right. There was no answer. It was useless. If Emma was inside, she didn't want to talk with anyone.

"She won't come to the door," the Cartright girl said, dismay tinging her voice.

"I tried to tell you that it was a waste of time going to see her."

Felicia sat down on the edge of the bed, hands tightly clasped. She wouldn't feel so bad if she had been faithful in presenting Christ to Emma. Silently, she asked forgiveness.

* * *

The following morning, the girls were still thinking about their distraught friend in the room next to theirs as they got ready to go down to breakfast.

"If we could just get to talk to Emma," Felicia said, "maybe we could help her."

"She might not want help," Joan reminded her. "Did you ever think of that?"

Felicia stopped what she was doing momentarily. "She might think she doesn't want help, but she needs help. That's enough for me."

"Here we go again," Joan muttered.

At Felicia's insistence, she finally agreed to wait with her in their room until they heard Emma leave for breakfast. Then they were to hurry and catch up with her.

"That way we can get to talking with her in the dining room," Felicia said. "We might be able to find out what's troubling her."

"If she goes to breakfast, that is," Joan remarked. "If she's as upset as she appears to be, she might not eat breakfast at all; and, if we wait on her, we'll be fasting until noon."

Felicia laughed, "I really don't think it would hurt either one of us to miss a meal."

"Speak for yourself, my dear. I'm a growing girl. I don't like to miss meals."

However, it wasn't long until they heard Emma stirring in her room; and, a short time before breakfast was to be served, she opened her door to go out.

"She's leaving now," Felicia hissed under her breath. "Hurry, Joan."

They managed to catch up with the girl before she reached the stairs.

"Oh, hello, Emma," Joan sang out.

Emma answered lifelessly.

"How about going to breakfast with us?" Felicia asked. "Or were you going to sit with someone else?"

Emma paused. The look in her eyes revealed that she didn't want to go to breakfast with anyone, but she was too gracious and polite to refuse.

"I am not so hungry this morning," she said. "At first, I think maybe I no go down to eat."

Felicia studied Emma's face as the three of them went down the stairs together. Her lips were compressed, and furrows of worry lined her forehead. There were dark, puffy circles beneath her eyes, the telltale shadows of much crying that showed through the carefully applied camouflage of makeup. Felicia saw, too, that Emma's black eyes were strangely luminous. Unshed tears still lurked beneath dark eyelashes.

On the other side, Joan was also studying Emma obliquely so she would not be aware of it. Felicia and Joan talked about events at school with forced cheerfulness in an effort to keep Emma from knowing that they had read the secret she was trying so hard to keep from them. Before they had finished breakfast, Joan, running out of conversation, launched into a detailed account of her current problems with English.

"You have trouble with English too?" Emma asked, finding difficulty in believing that such could be true. "It is your own language."

"It isn't Joan's language," Felicia said, laughing. "At least, what we study isn't her language."

Her friend stuck out the tip of her tongue at her. "That's not fair. I don't do as badly as all that."

"That's not what Miss Duncan says."

"Miss Duncan is just prejudiced."

Emma entered the conversation, trying desperately to act as happy and lighthearted as her companions. She talked about her own trouble with English and the difficulty she was having with American history. "Sometimes I think maybe your country do so many things just to cause trouble for those who have to study about it."

The other girls both laughed.

"That's one I've got to remember for Miss Duncan when she calls me in for grade trouble in history," Joan said.

Although Emma worked hard at it, Felicia and Joan could see that she wasn't really happy at all. It was part of the act to keep them from knowing how miserable she actually was.

As soon as she finished eating, she got quickly to her feet. "I have to go now. Thank you."

Joan stared at her. "Why are you thanking us?"

Emma smiled mysteriously and moved away.

It was two or three minutes before either Joan or Felicia spoke.

"If there was just some way we could help her," Felicia murmured, as much to herself as to her companion.

During the rest of the day, Joan spent as much time as possible on her English theme. When she didn't have class, she was in the library or up in their room working on it. That was probably the reason she forgot to lock her car after running a quick errand at noon. It was after dinner that night, and they were back in their room before she thought of it.

"Oh, bother!" she exclaimed aloud.

"What's the trouble now?" Felicia wanted to know.

"You wouldn't happen to be going out tonight, would you?"

Felicia's eyes gleamed curiously. "Not that anyone knows about. Why?"

"If you were going somewhere," Joan continued, "I thought maybe you wouldn't mind stopping on the way and locking my car."

"Don't tell me you've forgotten to lock your car again!" her friend exclaimed.

"It's only the third time this week," Joan said defensively.

"Maybe you won't have to lock it," Felicia told her. "Maybe it's been stolen."

"Spoken like a true and faithful friend who always looks on the good side of everything."

Without waiting for an answer, Joan got into her heavy coat. "I know you're not going to do it for me, so I'll have to do it myself, said the Little Red Hen."

She scurried down the stairs, buttoning her winter coat as she went.

Darkness came early in that part of the country during midwinter. The streetlights went on shortly after five o'clock, and, by six, it was as dark as midnight. Headlights stabbed twin holes in the gloom as cars crept along the icy street that fronted the Wellington School for Girls.

Joan stopped just inside the front door, surveying the scene before her.

New snow was beginning to fall, and the wind toyed with it. The rising breeze moved the snow briskly in narrow, twisting wisps along the crust of former snows. Momentarily, it would lie in the lee of a bush or a tree before another sudden gust wakened it and set it in motion again.

It was cold out there, Joan reasoned, as well as dark. Briefly she hesitated, wishing she had asked Felicia to come with her. She would have grumbled about it, but she would have gone with her. She always did. Joan knew that she could go back inside now and run up the stairs to get Felicia or call her to come down and go out to the parking lot with her. But, she told herself, that would be foolish. After all, it was only a short distance from the door to the parking lot. She could be out, have the car locked, and be back in the dorm again before Felicia would answer the phone.

Shivering, Joan tightened her collar around her throat and hurried out into the darkness.

She didn't know why, but she always felt uneasy about going out to the parking lot after dark. There was no reason for that, she told herself. She had done it a dozen times without any trouble. Still, she was strangely uneasy every time she had to walk across that narrow strip of pavement and along the building to the place where she parked her car.

Now that she was outside, she wished more than ever that she had asked Felicia to come with her. For an instant, she resisted an urge to turn and run back into the dorm and call her roommate.

"Now, wait a minute, Joan Bailey," she told herself aloud. "Don't get so worked up! You can't carry on like this just because it's dark."

It was only a hundred steps or so from the front door of the dormitory to the place where she parked her car. She stopped beside the little red convertible and started to lock the doors. At that instant, she heard a muffled footstep behind her – or thought she did. She jerked upright.

"I–" Fear choked her tense voice as she glanced wildly over her shoulder.

Joan caught a glimpse of a big, shadowy figure towering over her. She opened her lips to scream, but a powerful hand clamped over her mouth and nose. In the same quick movement, his other arm encircled her arms and waist and drew her back half a step. She kicked savagely with her heel.

"Ai!" The man's anguished voice echoed over the silent parking lot. She tried to kick again, but he tightened his hold on her.

Joan was trembling with terror but would not give up. She struggled to free herself, writhing against the force of the powerful arms that held her. But her struggling was useless. The man's steellike grip tightened until she could scarcely breathe. At last, she stopped fighting against him.

"I no hurt you!" he whispered hoarsely in a thick Spanish accent. "I no hurt. I want only for talk."

He loosened his grip slightly.

Joan Bailey weighed her chances to escape but decided it was impossible. Besides, he didn't act as though he was going to hurt her, at least for the moment.

"You go to that school for girls, no?" he continued.

Joan nodded.

"You know Emma Valdez?"

Her breath caught quickly. What could this person have to do with Emma?

"You know Emma Valdez?" The man's voice rose impatiently.

She did not answer.

"I know she go to school there. You give her this. Okay?" He thrust a wrinkled envelope into Joan's hand. "You give to Emma? Okay?"

With that, he released the Bailey girl with a little shove that thrust her off balance against the side of her car. It was a moment or two before she could right herself.

Numbly, Joan looked about. While the stranger had talked to her, she had been surprisingly calm; but, now that she was free, she was so terrified she could not move. It was all a wild dream. It wasn't true. It couldn't be. She would wake up in an instant or two, trembling, and find out that she was still in bed.

But, as she stood there, the cold was biting into her face and hands, and her fingers still clutched the crumpled envelope. She realized that it was true. Every terrifying moment of it. Her gaze swept the darkened parking lot with frantic haste, trying to catch a glimpse of the one who had grabbed her and thrust the envelope into her hand.

Her strength came back with a rush. She was able to move again. She forgot about locking her car and ran blindly across the parking lot toward the dormitory. At the edge of the paved drive, she caught her toe on the curb and went sprawling on the icy pavement. Shaken, Joan lay there for an instant, fighting for breath. Then she pushed herself up, scrambled to her feet, and dashed up the steps.

"Joan!" the receptionist gasped as she saw her, hands skinned and eyes wild. "Joan! What's the matter?"

The Bailey girl didn't even hear her. She hurried up the stairs and burst into the room where Felicia and Emma were sitting.

"Joan!" Felicia cried. "What on earth happened to you?"

"I–I–" Joan was breathing so heavily she could not go on.

"What is it?" Felicia cried. "What on earth happened to you?"

CHAPTER 4

THE QUESTIONING

Before Joan could reply to Felicia's frantic question, Miss Duncan came striding crisply into the room. She had been summoned by the frightened receptionist.

"Now, Miss Bailey," the dean of women began, her icy voice restoring calm and order, "would you please tell us what this is all about?"

While Joan was searching for words, the other girls on the floor pushed curiously into the room, staring at her.

Miss Duncan spun on a low, square heel and ordered them away. "This is no concern of yours, at least at the moment. A well-bred Wellington girl has control of her curiosity at all times." She shut the door decisively and locked it. Then she turned back to Joan and repeated her question.

"I–I was just going out to the car to lock it," she

began, stuttering over the words, "when this man came up behind me and–" Terror cut off her voice.

Miss Duncan's calm questioning quieted her.

"Now, you weren't hurt, Miss Bailey," she reminded her tautly. "There is no reason for you to be so upset. Just get control of yourself and tell me exactly what happened. What did he do?"

Joan told about his questioning her about Emma.

The color fled from the Cuban girl's cheeks, and she pressed her hand nervously over her lips.

Then Joan remembered the letter. "Oh, yes. He gave me this to give to you, Emma." She held out the soiled envelope.

Fear glittered in the girl's eyes. "For me?" Her hands were trembling as she held it.

Miss Duncan must have been disturbed, too, despite her outward display of calm, for it was not until then that she thought about the police.

"This is a matter for the authorities," she announced almost belligerently, as though she expected someone to give her an argument in the matter.

While Miss Duncan was gone, Emma opened the letter and began to read. She had only read a few lines when tears flooded her eyes.

Felicia, who had been watching her intently, moved closer. "What's the matter, Emma? Is there something wrong?"

Emma could not speak immediately. "It is of my Uncle Hermano," she stammered, her accent rushing back so thick they could scarcely understand her. "He–he is dead!"

Felicia put an arm around her comfortingly. She would have spoken, but what could one say at such a time as this?

Emma's shoulders shook. "Now I have nobody in America. I have nobody! I am all alone!"

"You have Joan and me," Felicia said softly, "and Miss Duncan and the other girls here at Wellington. We all love you!"

But Emma was not to be comforted. She was still crying when Miss Duncan sent for her and Joan.

"The police are here," the dean explained. "Please come down at once."

This was something else Emma could not understand. "The police?" she echoed. "We do nothing bad. Why the police come?"

Joan tried to explain to her that they had come in an effort to find the man who had accosted her in the parking lot. "They don't want to hurt us. They want to help."

"Help us?" Emma echoed, fear widening her eyes. "The police want to help us? No. It is not possible."

"You come down with me, and you'll soon see," Joan said. "I'm not afraid of them, and you don't have any reason to be afraid either."

Emma moved reluctantly in the direction of the door but stopped and turned back. "You come," she said to Felicia.

"But they don't want me."

"Please?" Dark eyes begged her to go along.

"All right. I'll go with you. And if Miss Duncan will allow me to stay, I'll stay while they talk with you."

The police detective questioned Joan first, asking her over and over again about every detail she could remember.

"I–I was so scared. I–I don't think I could describe him even if I had gotten a good look at him," Joan said frankly.

He nodded. "Can you give me some idea of how tall he was?"

"All I saw was a dark shape," she continued. "But, when I saw him an instant before he grabbed me, I'd have sworn that he was ten feet tall."

The officer laughed and made another notation in his book. Then he asked her to repeat the story with as much detail as possible. Every now and then, he stopped her to ask a clarifying question. At last, he seemed satisfied that he had all the information from Joan that she was able to supply.

"One more question," he said, closing his notebook. "Did you get the impression he wanted to harm you in any way?"

She shook her head. "When he first grabbed me I–I didn't know what was going to happen; but now that I think back on it, I believe all he wanted to do was to give me that letter for Emma Valdez."

At the mention of her name, Emma started to cry again.

"It does seem logical, in a way," the detective said, "but it poses problems too. If someone wanted to send a letter to Miss Valdez, why didn't he mail it to her? The mail is reliable and fast. Or he could have walked into the dormitory and asked the girl at the desk to see that she got the letter. Why would he feel that he had to do what he did just to put a letter in somebody's hands?"

Felicia and Joan eyed each other uneasily. What he said was true. That answer created as many new questions as it solved.

The officer turned to Emma. "Can you give us any help on that?" he asked quietly. "Can you explain why this man might not have wanted to use the mail or to show himself by appearing at the receptionist's desk to have her give you the letter?"

The Cuban girl shook her head mutely. Stark terror glinted in her eyes.

The detective saw it, and his manner softened. "We aren't going to hurt you. We just want to get the entire story so we can help you if we can."

He asked her another question or two, but it was as though she was suddenly struck dumb. Her eyes showed that she understood, but she did not speak.

At last, the officer motioned Miss Duncan to one side. "Is she always like this?"

"Quite the contrary. She's a highly intelligent girl

and is most cooperative in class and out." Pride crept into Miss Duncan's voice. "If you will pardon my saying so, Miss Valdez is a fine example of what we like to term our 'typical Wellington girl.'"

"She's terribly frightened or upset about something."

"It must be the death of her uncle. She was most fond of him." Miss Duncan hesitated, as though trying to decide whether or not to reveal some delicate bit of classified information. "In fact–" she lowered her voice markedly and leaned forward as though some unseen ear was straining to catch what she was about to say. "In fact, her uncle had placed her here in school and was paying her expenses, so you can see how close they were."

The officer pulled thoughtfully at his tie. "It's impossible to question her further now. I think I'll come back and talk with her in the morning."

When the detective was gone, Miss Duncan directed her attention to Felicia. "You girls have an extra bed in your room. "I am going to ask you to take Emma in with you, at least for tonight."

The Cuban girl smiled gratefully.

"And I think it best that you go now. It is already quite late."

In their room, Felicia and Joan tried to take Emma's mind off what had happened that night by talking about other things, but she insisted on bringing the conversation back to the visit of the authorities. She sat at Felicia's desk, her trembling hands constantly moving.

"This policeman," she began uneasily, "he come back tomorrow to talk to me, no?"

"That's right," Joan told her. "Miss Duncan and the detective thought you would feel more like answering questions in the morning."

Emma's concern grew. "These–these questions! What kind of questions they ask?"

Joan shrugged. "I don't have the slightest idea, but I suppose he'll want to know who that letter was from and what was in it so they can try to find out who grabbed me tonight."

Felicia saw fear leap into Emma's eyes. It was a wild, unreasoning fear that could not be quenched.

"What they do to me?" she asked numbly. With effort, she lifted her head to stare into Felicia's eyes. "They send me back to Cuba?"

"Of course not," Felicia told her. "That's the last thing they would do. Besides, you haven't broken the law."

For a moment that answer seemed to satisfy Emma; but, as she sat thinking about it, the fear flickered in her eyes again.

"One time you ask me how I get out of Cuba, but I no tell you." All of her poise was gone now, drained away by fear. "I–I no leave Cuba the way I should. My grandpa, he fight against the government, so they no let any of his family do nothing."

Emma paused, but it was apparent that she was going to continue as soon as she could.

"So he hire a boat that come after me at night. We sneak past the patrols and go to Miami." Her gaze fixed once more on Felicia. "They send me back, no?"

"I don't know anything about the law, but I'm sure they wouldn't do anything like that; especially if you went to the American authorities and registered the way you should."

"Right after I get to Miami, my Uncle Hermano, he take me someplace," Emma continued. "We go in this big building and talk to, oh so many people. He have me sign papers, and they give me this."

She opened the small purse she had brought into their room with her and removed a small card from it.

"This says you're registered as an alien," Felicia told her, studying the card. "You don't have anything to worry about. The American government isn't going to send you back to Cuba."

But Emma still was not satisfied. "The police, he ask so many questions."

"You don't have to worry about the police asking a lot of questions," Joan broke in. "They asked me a lot of questions, too, but that doesn't mean that they're going to do anything to us. Here in America, the police are for the protection of law-abiding citizens. As long as we haven't broken the law, we don't have to be afraid of them."

Emma folded a tissue into a neat little square,

pressing out the corners flat and smooth. It was a minute or two later before she looked up. "That policeman will want to read the letter?" Her voice was a thin whisper.

"I don't know," Felicia replied. "He may want to read it, and he may not."

The fear that had been smoldering in Emma's eyes flamed high. "Do I *have* to let them read it?"

Joan did not answer her question directly. "That's another thing you don't have to worry about, Emma. They will only want to read the letter because it may give them some information as to who to look for. They aren't going to tell anyone what's in it, and they aren't going to cause trouble for you because of it. If they do ask to see the letter, you don't have to worry about giving it to them."

Emma stopped her questioning as abruptly as she began. She settled back into her chair and lapsed into silence. The only way she revealed she was upset was by clutching the envelope as though she was terrified that it would somehow get out of her possession.

The girls continued to talk with her until finally Felicia glanced at the clock on her desk.

"We're going to have to turn out the lights in a few minutes," she said, reaching for her Bible. "Would you like to join us for our devotions before we go to bed, Emma?"

The girl got to her feet. "Sí, I come back in one

minute for these–these devotion. I go to my room now."

When she was gone, Joan turned to Felicia and whispered, "Did you ever see anyone so afraid of the authorities? She acts as though she expects the police to throw her into jail for a hundred years or so."

Felicia nodded. "I wondered about that, too, but I got to thinking that maybe we would be the same way if we lived in a place like she did and had to live in fear of the authorities all the time."

"I'd never thought of that."

"From what I understand," Felicia went on, "it doesn't seem to make any difference in Cuba whether you've broken the law or not. If they think you're against the government, they're likely to arrest you without any reason at all and throw you in jail."

Joan started to reply, but stopped and sniffed the air. "Do you smell anything?"

"It smells like something's burning."

The two girls went out into the hall. The odor of smoke was stronger there.

"I'll ring the alarm!" Joan cried.

But Felicia stopped her. "Wait!" She held up a hand in warning. "I think it's coming from Emma's room!"

CHAPTER 5

A BURNED LETTER

Felicia dashed over and tried the door to the room Emma had gone into moments before. Smoke was curling up from under it.

"Emma!" she cried. "Emma! Are you all right?"

"One moment!"

"What is wrong in there?"

For answer, Emma opened the door. Smoke filled her little room.

"What is it?" Joan demanded.

By this time, heads were popping out of doors along either side of the corridor.

"There is nothing the matter now." A thin note of triumph edged the girl's voice. "The fire is out now."

Felicia and Joan went into her room and closed the door behind them, much to the dismay of the other girls who were looking on.

"What was burning?" Felicia asked.

In answer to her question, Emma picked up the metal wastebasket at her feet and showed them the charred remnants of several sheets of paper. A slender spiral of smoke still twisted up from them.

"What did you do?" Felicia asked.

"Now I no have to worry about the police reading the letter!" she informed them. "Now they no find out what was in it."

Felicia shook her head. How could they make her understand that she had nothing to fear from the authorities? Felicia didn't know what the detective was going to say when he learned that Emma had destroyed the letter the man asked Joan to deliver to her. She had an idea that he was going to be awfully mad.

The fact that the letter was gone seemed to set Emma completely at ease. She sat quietly through devotions and even bowed her head when Joan prayed.

The following morning when Miss Duncan sent for Emma to come down to her office for questioning by the police detective, the girl insisted that Felicia and Joan go with her.

"But Miss Duncan asked for you to come. She didn't say that we should be with you."

"I want you with me," she said firmly.

Joan glanced at Felicia. "What do you think?"

"The worst that can happen is that she'll kick us out."

The dean of women met Joan and Felicia at the

door. "I sent for Miss Valdez," she informed them curtly.

"She wanted us to be with her."

"That won't be necessary. Miss Valdez has nothing to fear from either myself or Detective Powers." Her gaze wandered to the clock on the wall. "And you both should be in class."

Emma stared at them helplessly, but there was nothing they could do to change the situation. Miss Duncan had dismissed them. They had to stay dismissed.

"I feel so sorry for her," Felicia said as she and her roommate went down the hall. "She wanted us to be with her while she talked to Mr. Powers. I don't know if I've ever seen anyone so frightened."

"She may be frightened," Joan said, "but she's sharp enough to think ahead all the time."

"You mean about burning that letter?"

Joan nodded. "Who else do you know who would *dare* to do a thing like that?"

Felicia smiled thoughtfully. "She acts to me as though she's going to be able to take care of herself."

At the door to the room where they had their first class of the day, they paused.

"There's something else that seems strange to me," Felicia said in tones little above a whisper. "Did you notice how hard she took the death of her uncle?"

"I hadn't thought about it," Joan said, "but now

that you mention it, she was awfully shaken up over the death of an uncle."

"Of course, he may have been awfully close to her family."

"It didn't sound that way when she was telling Miss Duncan she hadn't heard from him. I got the impression he didn't write very often. Yet, she cried and carried on over his death as though she had lost one of her parents."

Joan thought about that for a time.

"When I consider everything that's happened since Emma came here to school, it makes me wonder if there is something else behind all of this – something we don't know anything about." A frown briefly wrinkled Felicia's forehead.

"What do you mean?" Joan asked, her own concern feeding on that of her friend. "Do you think Emma might be in on something that–that isn't honest?"

Felicia spoke slowly. "I don't know how she could be. She's a sweet girl and seems so well-mannered and everything. I just can't believe she'd be mixed up with anything that was crooked."

Joan nodded her agreement. "But you've got to admit that none of us know anything about her at all. She showed up at school and was taken in. Actually, she could be almost anyone."

"I'm not going to believe it until I have to," Felicia said. "I'm sure she's not that sort of a girl."

"I'd hate to believe it myself." But Joan's voice left

the sentence dangling, as though she could believe almost anything about Emma Valdez if it was accompanied by a bit of evidence.

Felicia and Joan had hoped that Emma would be coming along before they had to go into the classroom, but the bell sounded. Mr. Powers had not yet finished questioning their friend. So, it was not until noon that they were able to talk with her. She came into the dining room slowly, eyes searching for them.

"Oh, there she is!" Felicia exclaimed, standing.

Emma's eyes lighted as she saw her friends, and she hurried over to them. "I am so glad you are here. I was afraid I have missed you."

"How did you make out with the police?" Joan asked. "Was he nice to you?"

"Sí." Emma's smile played hide and seek with the corners of her mouth. "He do not like it that I have burn the letter, but he do nothing about it."

"We tried to tell you that you didn't have anything to worry about."

"Our police aren't unreasonable," Felicia added. "And they have to live up to the law. Even if the officer wanted to arrest you, he couldn't unless he had a good reason for it."

This seemed difficult for Emma to understand. She looked from one attractive young face to the other.

"What about the character who grabbed me and scared me half to death?" Joan wanted to know. "Have they caught him yet?"

"He says they look and look, but they no find anybody." She seemed relieved about that too. Almost as relieved as she was that the authorities hadn't pressed her any harder about the letter she burned.

"I can't understand it," Joan said when she and Felicia were alone once more. "If somebody had grabbed a friend of mine the way that man grabbed me, I'd want him arrested. I wouldn't care if he had sent me a letter from a relative."

"Almost anybody would." Felicia's eyes narrowed. "There are a lot of things about Emma that we don't know."

The affair of the letter seemed to bring Emma closer to Felicia and Joan than anything else. She asked them to sit with her at dinner that night and came into their room later when they were studying. For half an hour or so, she sat there uneasily.

At last, Felicia saw that she was still troubled. "Can we help you with something, Emma?"

Their visitor looked up and then away quickly, as though afraid to have them peer too deeply into her eyes.

Felicia repeated her question.

"I come to ask you something," she said truthfully, "but, now I am here, it seem so–so–how you say? So foolish."

"You shouldn't feel that way," Felicia replied. "Go ahead and ask. We won't think it's foolish."

Emma was fidgeting with a pen. "When I am

here last night after–after I burn the letter, you have the Bible reading and–" She paused, searching for words. "And–and then you pray."

"Yes?"

It was hard for Emma to go on. "You do this again tonight?"

"We read the Bible and have prayer together every night," Joan put in. "Why?"

"I am think maybe when you talk to God you–you ask Him about this–this thing I have to decide."

Now, it was out! She squinted narrowly at the girls. It seemed to Felicia that Emma's brown cheeks lightened noticeably and her lips trembled. She started to speak again but stopped helplessly.

"We'll be glad to pray for you," Felicia told her. "Why don't we pray about it now – while you're here?"

Emma's smile was genuine.

They bowed their heads in prayer. Felicia was first, and then Joan, asking God to guide Emma in the decision she had to make. When they finished, their visitor stood.

"Gracias," she said, lapsing into her own language momentarily. "Gracias, amigas."

She started for the door, but Felicia called her back.

"There's something I've been wanting to talk with you about. You believe in prayer, so I know you believe in God."

"Sí." Emma spoke simply, but with disarming

directness. "Sí. All my family believe in God. Every Sunday we go to church, when we can."

"That's fine, but have you ever considered Christ's claim on your life?"

Questions gleamed in Emma's eyes. "What you mean, Christ's claim on my life? I go to church. I do what I am suppose to do."

"The Bible says that all have sinned and come short of the glory of God," Felicia went on, "and that the wages of sin is death. So, we've all sinned, and we all deserve to be sent to hell."

Emma grew very serious as she considered that. She nodded in agreement but added, "What about the claim Christ have for me?"

"He died on the cross and rose again so we could confess our sin and be saved."

Emma turned the matter over in her mind. "I think on it. Gracias."

With that, she swept from the room, leaving Felicia and Joan alone once more.

"Now, what do you make of that?" Joan asked.

"I don't know," Felicia murmured. "I'm more perplexed now than ever."

The next morning, Emma was quiet and reflective, but she did not mention her request for prayer or their conversation about her personal relationship with Christ. In fact, a week went by, and she said nothing more about those things or the strange events that had taken place.

"If it wasn't that she is so quiet," Felicia observed, "I'd begin to wonder if all of this was actually real."

"It was real, all right," Joan said, shuddering, "I still wake up in the middle of the night with cold chills, dreaming that man has grabbed me again."

Everything at Wellington School for Girls went smoothly the next few days. It was not apparent to the students that the police were still keeping the school under surveillance. Even Felicia and Joan, who were very conscious of what had taken place, almost forgot about it. They didn't go out alone, not to the parking lot or even to the library at night – that was the chief difference. They pushed the matter to the backs of their minds, almost as though it had never happened, and went about their regular school activities. For once, Joan had all of her grades up and had no extra studies to do. For the next two weeks, all was as quiet as ever around the school.

And then it happened.

Midnight came and went, and the dormitory was locked in the silence of sleep when a sudden, terrified scream shattered the quiet.

"Joan!" Felicia cried, jerking herself to an upright position. "Joan! Did you hear that?"

The scream came again, shrill and piercing. This time it seemed to originate in the room next to theirs.

"Emma!" Joan leaped out of bed, grabbed her robe, and dashed for the door of their friend's room.

Felicia was half a step behind her as they burst into the room.

"Emma!" Joan repeated the name. "Emma! Are you all right?"

At first, the girls couldn't see her and, for a terrifying instant, were afraid she had been whisked away.

"Emma!" Felicia repeated, fumbling for the light switch.

She found it and flicked it upward, flooding the room with light. Emma was sitting in the middle of her bed, lips parted slightly and a trembling hand pointing in the general direction of the window.

"What is it?" Joan demanded.

By this time, other girls on the floor were crowding into the room, staring mutely at Emma.

"What is it?" Felicia asked, her voice rising.

Still Emma could not force herself to speak.

"She must have seen something over there," Joan said. "That's the direction she's been pointing ever since we came in here."

Felicia went over to the window. Someone had cut the screen, and the sash was open six or seven inches although it was bitter cold outside.

"Look, Joan," Felicia gasped, her voice trembling. "Somebody tried to break in!"

CHAPTER 6

THE MESSAGE IS REVEALED

The girls who had crowded into Emma's room all found voice at the same time. They pushed close to the window, pointing at the slit screen and the open sash, and babbled to each other in their excitement.

Only Emma was silent. A deathlike pallor robbed the glow from her cheeks, and her slight figure was still curled on the bed in the same way she had been when Felicia and Joan burst into the room moments before. She stared numbly into space as though she suddenly had been robbed of speech.

Felicia could not force her gaze away from the terrified girl. She wanted to put an arm around Emma and try to comfort her, but she would have felt strange doing that in front of the others. Emma was as old as she was.

At that moment, Miss Duncan, looking even more severe than ever in her corduroy robe and scraggly hair, forced her way into the crowd.

"Girls!" Her voice was like a saw, harsh and rasping. "Just what is going on here?"

Talk cut off suddenly, as though Miss Duncan had thrown a switch.

In the taut silence that followed, her withering gaze sought one youthful face and then another. The girls cringed under her cold stare as girls at the school had been doing for more than fifteen years.

"I would appreciate an explanation of this uproar," she demanded. "You all know that at Wellington, girls are in bed and presumably asleep by ten o'clock."

Felicia was the one who answered her. She pointed a wavering finger at the slash in the screen. "Look!"

Now it was Miss Duncan's turn to gasp. In spite of her Wellington self-control, she paled noticeably. When she spoke, her voice trembled. "Who did this?"

The sound of the dean of women's voice seemed to break the bonds that held Emma's tongue.

"I–I hear a noise out there," she began. "It was a not-so-loud noise, but it woke me up. At first, I no see anything, but then I see this–this dark figure out there and the hand lifting the window." She shuddered and gave evidence of going into shock again. "It was terrible!"

By this time, Miss Duncan had regained her composure. "I'm sure it was a trying experience, but that is no reason for you to lose control of yourself."

Emma nodded weakly.

In the silence that followed, Miss Duncan directed

her attention to the other girls. "There is no need for the rest of you to be in here. Whoever was at the window was frightened away. He won't be coming back tonight, so there is no need for your concern."

The girls eyed each other uneasily.

"Please go to your rooms at once."

There was a moment's hesitation.

"And remember, lights are to be out immediately, and there is to be no talking."

"But, Miss Duncan!" a frightened student murmured.

"Do as I say."

Reluctantly, they began to file out into the corridor, still mumbling to one another guardedly.

Emma turned pleadingly to Miss Duncan. "I–I can't stay in here alone, Miss Duncan." She was trembling on the brink of hysteria.

The dean of women softened noticeably. "Of course, you can't, my dear. I wouldn't expect you to, although we will alert the authorities, and they will keep a close watch on the school for the rest of the night." Miss Duncan paused, as though wondering what to do about Emma. "You may go to Miss Cartright and Miss Bailey's room," she informed her.

The girl smiled gratefully.

"I would suggest, however, that you get dressed immediately. I am sure the police will want to question you tonight."

Emma jerked upright. "Again?"

"Again," Miss Duncan repeated. "And this time, they probably will be more persistent than before."

That bit of information seemed to upset Emma more than the fact that a man had tried to break into her room, if that were possible. Her shoulders trembled violently, and her eyes overflowed with tears.

"I cannot do it," she told Felicia and Joan when the dean of women had gone to phone the police. "I no talk to him again."

"You'll have to."

"You go with me, no?" She grasped Felicia's arm in desperation. "You go with me?"

"I'd like to, but I'm afraid Miss Duncan wouldn't approve."

"That's putting it mildly," Joan said. "Miss Duncan would blow a gasket if we showed up with you in her office."

Emma frowned, and the girls were afraid she was going to start to cry again.

"I talk to Miss Duncan," she said firmly, at last. "I go now and call her."

She went out to the hall. A moment later, she was back, triumph in her eyes. "She say you come," she announced. "Only you be quiet about it, so other girls not know."

Joan shook her head, muttering, "I don't get it. Every time I'm sure Miss Duncan is made of stone, she does something to make me wonder if she is human after all."

Mr. Powers came to the school a few minutes after Miss Duncan phoned him. He was kind in his questioning of Emma yet stern and insistent.

"This matter is most serious, Miss Valdez," he began, his bleak stare boring into her. "I hope you appreciate the fact that anyone who would try to do what this man tried to do tonight is capable of almost anything."

A tremor ran up Emma's slim frame.

"This time he failed, but the next time he might succeed in getting into your room. Do you understand?"

"Sí." She nodded gravely.

"You are going to have to answer every question and give us every scrap of information you have if we are going to be able to help you."

Emma folded her hands in a futile attempt to keep them from trembling.

The detective's face grew stern. "If you had not burned the letter you received, we probably could have gained enough information from it to have arrested the persons responsible." He paused to give her time to understand the significance of what he was saying. "We could have avoided this incident tonight."

"I–I am sorry," she replied. "I–" Fear stole her words.

"Let's start at the very beginning. Who wrote that letter and exactly what did it say?"

The lump in her throat grew, and she swallowed against it.

"Who wrote it?" he repeated firmly.

"It–it was from my Uncle Hermano," she told him.

"Your uncle?" The lines across his forehead deepened. "Now, wait a minute. You told us that letter notified you of his death."

"Sí."

"I'd like an explanation of that, please," he said icily.

"He–" she was more frightened than ever now that she was forced to reveal the information that was in the letter. "He was in a group that try to make Cuba free and–"

Mr. Powers' lips tightened. "I thought it might be something like that," he murmured to himself.

"He knew that the–the government agents were after him, and so he write me this letter. He give it to one of the men who help him and tell him to give it to me if–if something happen to him. You understand?"

The detective nodded, eyes gleaming. "And it was this man who grabbed Miss Bailey in the parking lot a couple of weeks ago?"

"Sí."

Felicia studied the Cuban girl obliquely. That explained a number of things she had been wondering about. Still, there were many questions that were unanswered.

"Did your uncle say why he thought he would be killed?" the detective asked. "Was he a leader of this resistance group?"

She shook her head. "He work in it. My grandfather

in Cuba work in it, too, but I do not know about this leader. All I know is he say he have to go back to Cuba, and it is most dangerous for him to do that. He think maybe they catch him this time."

"You're sure he went back to Cuba?"

"No–" Her eyes pleaded that she was telling the truth. "I only say that he tell me he go back to Cuba. I not know if he do it."

"I see." Mr. Powers changed his line of questioning abruptly. "Would you mind looking at some pictures, Miss Valdez? Tell us if the man in them is your uncle."

"Sí."

He took them from his pocket and handed them to her.

Her eyes widened. "Where you get? Where you get these pictures?"

"Do you recognize the man?"

"Sí. It is Uncle Hermano. Only–"

"Only *what?*"

"He looks so–so different."

"These are the pictures of a man whose body washed ashore near Key West, Florida, a couple of weeks ago."

"The man is Uncle Hermano," she repeated numbly. "I knew he was dead." Her voice tightened. "I knew they not bring me the letter if he no dead."

There was another long silence while the detective searched Emma's face questioningly. "I won't bother you anymore tonight, Miss Valdez, but we may come to you later for a statement concerning your uncle. With your help, we might be able to locate the men who killed him if they are in the United States."

"Gracias," she murmured, eyes filling with tears. "Gracias."

Mr. Powers thanked Emma for her help, talked briefly with Miss Duncan, and left. All the while, the Cuban girl sat there crying silently.

Miss Duncan allowed her to cry for a time before telling Felicia and Joan to take her upstairs. "And thank you both," the dean of women said. "I am so grateful for your help and concern for Miss Valdez, and I know she is too."

Emma said nothing more until they were back in their room with the door shut and locked. She stumbled and grasped Joan's arm to right herself.

"Emma! Are you all right?"

"Sí." She still clung to her friend desperately. "I–I think so."

"You'd better sit down over here."

Joan and Felicia helped her across the room to a chair. She was no longer crying but was trembling violently.

"What is it, Emma?" Felicia bent over her.

"Maybe she needs a doctor," Joan exclaimed. "I'll get Miss Duncan!"

At the mention of the dean of women, Emma jerked upright. "No!" Her voice spat out the word. "No! I am all right! Okay! Understand?"

The girls pulled up chairs and sat down close by.

"What is wrong, Emma?" Felicia repeated, her voice a thin whisper.

"Is there anything we can do to help you?"

"Uncle Hermano say I no tell anyone, but he is–is dead now and I–" Emma's voice trailed away into silence as she fought within herself.

"Perhaps it would be good for you to tell someone so you can get help."

"Sí. I think maybe it is good." Emma sighed deeply. "I am so tired of hiding things."

"You mean you didn't tell Mr. Powers the truth?" Felicia asked. "You hid things from him?"

Emma hesitated, looking from one to the other. "I no keep things from him the way you think. I tell him all I know about Uncle Hermano, and I answer everything he ask." Her voice caught. "But, what he no ask, I no tell him."

"I see."

"And now you think you should tell us," Joan said. "Is that right?"

"Sí." It was not easy for her to go on. "You no tell anyone?"

"We won't tell anyone," Felicia assured her.

"Nothing?"

"We won't tell anyone anything you don't want us to tell."

That seemed to satisfy Emma.

"In old Cuba, my family have plenty of money,"

she began. "Two big houses–" She held up two fingers for emphasis. "Big boat for fishing and sleeping on and so many helpers." She spread out the fingers on one hand. "We have cook for cooking, maid for cleaning and washing, gardener for taking care of the yard, and two employees for–" She paused, shrugging as though it didn't matter anymore what the other two employees did. "For good times, my mama go to Miami or Switzerland skiing, even. And, when I am little, we go everywhere we want in our boat."

Felicia glanced at Joan. They had been sure Emma Valdez was used to having a great deal of money and everything she wanted. Now they knew it to be true.

"Now," Emma continued," we have nothing in Cuba. Everything our family owns have been take away and I–" Her voice caught. "I have to leave Wellington at the end of the month."

"You have to leave?" Joan echoed. "But why? Is your family making you go?"

"It is not that. I have no money to pay the school. Uncle Hermano was suppose to come back and pay more, but now he is dead. The school let me stay for long time without making the pay, but now they say I no can stay longer. I have to leave."

"We can't let them do that to you," Joan blurted. "We'll talk to Miss Duncan and get her working on it. She won't let them turn you away."

"Miss Duncan do what she can," Emma went on. "She write many letters trying to find someone who help me, but she no find anyone to pay for me." Forcibly, Emma pushed back the tears. "It is no use. I have to go."

Felicia studied the girl's somber face.

"Where will you go?"

Emma shrugged expressively but did not answer her.

"Do you have any friends here in America?"

Emma shook her head. "Only here at school."

"What will you do?" Felicia persisted.

"Get a job someplace, maybe." Fear tinged the other girl's voice. "Only I have never work any place before. Always people do things for me. I not know what I can do for to earn money."

Felicia breathed deeply. The situation was even worse than she had supposed it to be. What could a girl like Emma do, who had been waited on for most of her life?

"What was the information in the letter that you didn't tell the police?" Joan asked suddenly, breaking the tense silence.

Emma glanced over her shoulder, lowering her voice in fear. "He say he is sorry he have so little for me. He say my grandfather always say they see I have plenty for to go to school, but he not know about that now."

Felicia could not mask her disappointment. "Is that all that was in the letter?"

Emma hesitated. "There was something else, only I not know what it mean."

"Yes?" The girls leaned forward intently.

"He write something about my grandfather that I no understand. He say my grandfather think so much of America he want to do something for her. He send word that he try."

Felicia was breathing slowly, thoughtfully. "That is unusual. What could your grandfather do for our country?"

Emma shrugged. "I not know. I not know how I can help either."

"What do you mean?"

"He say my grandfather send word that I have to help."

"You?" Joan blurted incredulously. "But how?"

"He say I know when time comes."

This was a new development. It scarcely seemed possible that an aging Cuban could help America or that his granddaughter could have a part in it. Yet, somehow, Felicia believed their new friend. This wasn't the sort of story a person would make up, as incredible as it sounded.

"Was there anything else in the letter?" Joan asked.

"Nothing," Emma replied, "except the key."

Felicia and Joan gasped. "The key?" they echoed. "What kind of a key?"

"Only a key," Emma said. "It was not anything special. At least he no say anything about it."

Felicia pursed her lips thoughtfully. A key in a letter like that was strange indeed.

CHAPTER 7

A MYSTERIOUS KEY

Felicia's gaze sought the dark eyes of their Cuban companion and held there. That key had to be important, or it wouldn't have been included in the letter to Emma from her Uncle Hermano. Felicia was positive of that. But what was it for? And why didn't the letter say anything about it?

Or had it?

"Are you sure the letter didn't mention the key?" she asked. "Could it have said something that you missed, Emma?"

That must be it. The girl had been so upset when she got the letter revealing her uncle's death and had been so afraid the police were going to put her in jail that she hadn't read all of the letter carefully. There had been a reference to the key, and she had missed it.

But Emma was sure that she had not missed anything in the letter. "No, it not say anything about a key. I not know what it is for." It really didn't make any difference now whether there had been any mention of the key in Uncle Hermano's letter or not. It had been destroyed.

"Could we see the key?" Joan asked.

Emma went into the other room and came back with it moments later.

Joan turned it over in her fingers, examining it closely. "It looks like a locker key of some sort."

Felicia peered over her shoulder. It did look like the key to a locker somewhere. "What's the lettering on it?"

Her roommate held the key in the light and squinted at it. "'Alpine Ski Lodge,'" she read aloud. "That's on this side. And number 51 is on the other side."

"Hmmm," Felicia murmured. "It sounds to me as though your uncle had a locker at this Alpine Ski Lodge, wherever it is, and has something important stashed away there."

Joan nodded, still turning the key between her thumb and forefinger. "That ought to narrow down the search a lot. There are only scads of Alpine Ski Lodges all over. Who's going to know which one Emma's Uncle Hermano has a locker at?"

Felicia was silent for a moment. "Let me take a look at that key again."

"There's nothing more on it," Joan said, holding it out to her. "It looks as though there was another name or something on it, but it's been worn off."

Still, Felicia examined the key with care. "There was some other name on here, and it was fairly short. But it's gone now."

Emma sighed. "I not know why Uncle Hermano send key to me and no say what it is for or where it is even."

Joan got restlessly to her feet. "If we just had a list of the ski lodges around here, it would help. At least we'd know how many named Alpine there are."

Felicia jerked upright. "That's it, Joan!"

Her friend's eyes widened. "What are you talking about?"

"The Ski Lodge Association placed a directory of lodges in the library. I remember seeing it there last week."

"Sí," Emma spoke up. "I see him, too. I think about it because my mama, she like to ski so well when she is alive."

"What good will that do us?" Joan wanted to know.

"We can check it for the lodges that use the word Alpine in their name," Felicia continued. "At least we can find out how big a job we would have in running them down."

* * *

The following day, as soon as she had a free period, Felicia hurried over to the library and checked out the Ski Lodge Directory.

"Planning a skiing trip, eh?" the librarian asked.

"Right now, I'm interested in checking the names of some ski lodges," Felicia explained.

"If you want the name of an ideal place to go, come to me. We've been going to the same lodge for years. The rates are reasonable, and the skiing is fabulous."

The librarian sounded as though she could continue for half an hour, but Felicia thanked her and assured her that if she planned a ski trip, she would see her first.

Emma and Joan were waiting breathlessly for their friend in their room at the dorm.

"Did you get it?"

"I went after it, didn't I?" she remarked. "Of course, I got it."

She opened the directory on the desk, and her companions crowded close, staring over her shoulders. Felicia had thought the lodges would be indexed alphabetically, but they were indexed by regions instead.

"The chances are this particular ski lodge is close by," Joan muttered.

"I wouldn't be too sure of that," Felicia said. "Actually, there's no knowing where Uncle Hermano would have been or where he would have hidden anything in a locker. If it's something important, he might have deliberately chosen a place that's some distance from here, just to throw off guard anyone who might be nosing around."

"You're going to be a lot of help," Joan said under her breath. "As if we don't have enough Alpine Ski Lodges to check out now."

She ran her finger down the list.

"'Majestic Alpine Ski Lodge,'" Joan read aloud, "'Ed's Alpine Ski Lodge,' 'Bill and Norma's Alpine Ski Lodge.'" She flipped the pages to another regional listing a little farther from the school and called out the names that used the word Alpine in them.

Emma groaned aloud. "There are so many! Never we find the right one."

At first, Felicia shared the same feeling of frustration. They would never be able to check out all the possibilities. But, she reasoned, would they have to? She was beginning to get an idea.

"That key looks old," she said aloud.

"It would have to be," Joan countered. "Part of the lettering has been worn off, it's been handled so much."

"I hadn't thought of that," Felicia went on. "That means we can eliminate all the new lodges, regardless of their names."

Joan studied the key once more. "It's got to be a short name, too. There isn't room enough for anything very long, the way the rest of the lettering is arranged."

"That narrows it down still further."

Emma only partially understood what they were saying, but she did grasp the fact that they thought there might be some way of helping her locate Uncle Hermano's locker and find out what was in it.

"Maybe we find, eh?" she echoed.

"We can narrow it down to two or three," Felicia said, "and have the police try to locate the locker and find out what's in it."

At the mention of the authorities, Emma leaped to her feet, fear blazing in her dark eyes. "No police! No police!"

"But, Emma," Felicia protested, "they won't hurt you. You were afraid of them before, and they didn't do anything to you."

However, the frightened girl acted as though she did not hear her. "No police!" She grasped frantically for the key. "We no give it to police."

"If we don't get the help of the authorities," Joan said, "how will we check out the lodges we decide are likely prospects?"

"I want you to go with me," Emma announced firmly. "You I trust."

Felicia and Joan stared bleakly at one another. This was something they hadn't counted on. They could not go running from one ski lodge to another looking for a locker that might or might not exist. It was unthinkable. Miss Duncan would never permit it.

"You go with me." There was a note of helplessness and pleading in her voice. "No?"

"We'd be glad to go with you," Felicia said, "but

we don't know whether we can or not. Miss Duncan probably wouldn't let us."

"I talk to her," Emma announced firmly. "First, I get her promise that she no tell *anyone*. Then I talk to her."

Felicia and Joan insisted that Emma talk with Miss Duncan first – before they were even in her office.

"We want her to know that the idea is yours," Joan said. "Not ours."

After a few moments with Emma, the dean of women called her secretary on the intercom and had her send in Felicia and Joan. She did not speak until the office door had closed behind them and they were seated.

"I have just been explaining to Miss Valdez," she began, looking from one to the other, "that I quite appreciate the position she finds herself in and wish it was within my power to make it possible for her to stay here at Wellington. But, after the events of the last two weeks, I would be remiss in my responsibilities to your parents and to you if I were to allow the three of you to go off somewhere without proper chaperonage by some member of the faculty."

Joan seized upon her explanation. "Does that mean you would let us go if there was someone to go along with us?"

"I didn't say that," Miss Duncan replied.

But to someone like Joan, it was an opening – an

opportunity to drive in a wedge against the dean of women's announced decision.

"But you did say that the only reason you didn't want us to go was because we might be in danger without a faculty member to look after us. Isn't that right?"

Miss Duncan knew she was making a fatal admission to Joan, but that did seem to be a reasonable paraphrasing of her words. There wasn't any other valid reason for not recognizing the request.

"Then why don't you come with us?"

"Me?" Miss Duncan's eyes widened, and it was only with effort that she was able to maintain her proper Wellington manner. "I don't see how I could."

"We wouldn't have to be away from school more than two or three days," Felicia put in. "And it *might* mean that Emma – I mean Miss Valdez – would be able to remain at Wellington. And you know how much that would mean to all of us."

The dean of women weakened slightly. "There are to be two days of tests next week," she said, "followed by a day of vacation. You probably could make arrangements with your instructors to take those tests ahead of time."

"Then you will go with us?" Joan asked.

Miss Duncan stiffened. "I do not like to have words placed in my mouth, Miss Bailey," she said, growing even more stern than usual. "All I am agreeing to do is to think about it and look into the matter. I'll have to examine my own schedule to see if it would be possible for me to get away. Then I would have to contact my assistant, Miss Walters, to see if she is going to be available to look after things while I am away. Once that is accomplished, I shall make my decision. And only then. Is that clear?"

"Yes, Miss Duncan."

The dean of women stood abruptly, closing the interview. "I shall be in touch with you."

"Sí," Emma murmured. "Gracias, Señorita Duncan."

In their room, she turned to her American friends. "You think she go with us, no?" Her voice betrayed her uneasiness.

"It's hard to say what Miss Duncan will do," Joan replied. "She makes up her own mind."

Emma was quiet for a time. At last, she turned to Felicia. "You pray for me that Miss Duncan say she go with us so we can go to see about this key, no?"

"Of course, we will."

"You are good friends," Emma said seriously. "You are very good friends." Her smile was as warm as her country's sun.

When they finished praying, Felicia went back to the Ski Lodge Directory, writing down the names of those lodges that Uncle Hermano might have visited.

"I don't know why you're wasting your time with that," Joan said. "We don't even know if we're going to be able to go."

"I know that, but we've got to be ready just in case."

The task was difficult. They read the descriptions of the various lodges and tried to figure out which were new and which were old. In some cases, it was simple. In others, they could not be sure. The lodges sounded new or old, but they realized they were making decisions on the basis of the way certain words were used, and that might or might not give them the correct answers.

"I don't know what to do about this one," Felicia exclaimed, scribbling the name and address on the sheet. "I'm going to mark it with a big, fat question mark."

"If Miss Duncan agree to go with us," Emma asked, "what we do then?"

Felicia noted the number of lodges on her list. It was obvious that they would never be able to visit all of them.

"How we find the right ski lodge?" Emma persisted.

"That's what I've been trying to figure out," Felicia said thoughtfully. "But, when you ask it that way, I've got to admit that I simply don't know."

CHAPTER 8

SEARCH FOR LOCKER 51

For the next several days, the girls heard nothing from Miss Duncan about the proposed trip.

Every afternoon, Emma would inquire about it seriously. "What you think, Felicia? You think we get to go?"

At first, Felicia had been quite certain Miss Duncan would make arrangements to accompany them. She was most concerned about the fact that Emma was going to have to leave school and had no one to stay with to look after her. She knew that Miss Duncan would go to great lengths to look after one of her girls.

But, when several days passed without word from the dean of women, she began to wonder. It wasn't like Miss Duncan to postpone a decision. She always claimed that decisiveness was a characteristic of the ideal Wellington girl.

"I just don't know," Felicia told Emma thoughtfully.

As it was, Miss Duncan did not notify them directly. Instead, the English instructor had the three of them stay after class.

"Miss Duncan informs me that you girls will be absent on the day the rest of the class will be taking our tests," Miss Winthrop said, "so I am going to ask you to come in tomorrow after school prepared to take the test."

The girls looked at one another quickly, stunned by the implication of the teacher's information.

"We get to go after all!" Emma exclaimed, so excited her voice raised loudly. "Miss Duncan decided to go with us to look about the ski lodge!"

"You'd better pipe down if you don't want everybody else in school to know about it," Joan warned under her breath.

Emma's cheeks flushed, and, aware of what she had done, she glanced around uneasily as though to see if she had been overheard. She lowered her voice to a whisper. "Sí, sí, I try to be quiet, but it is hard when I am so excite."

"We know just what you mean," Felicia told her. "We both feel the same way about it."

After they had taken their tests, Miss Duncan called them in, affirmed her decision to go with them, and went over the list of ski lodges that they had prepared. She asked a few questions about their preparation of the list and how they decided to eliminate any given ski resort. Felicia and Joan both tried to explain to her.

"It looks to me as though you have done an excellent job," she commended. For the moment, she strummed her desk thoughtfully with a pen. "We probably could lessen the time the search will take by using the telephone, but I'm not entirely sure that's wise. So, we'll go about it as you have planned."

Before the three girls left her office, she informed them that they would plan to leave Wellington as soon as breakfast was over.

"And," she cautioned, "I shouldn't have to warn you against talking loosely about this. We must not forget that someone tried to break into Miss Valdez's room a few nights ago. I am sure there is no reason for concern, but we must always be alert in possibly dangerous situations."

They were just leaving the office of the dean of women when a police officer strode into the building hurriedly.

"Are you Miss Duncan?" he demanded.

"That's right."

He started to speak but glanced at the girls and checked himself. "May I see you in private?"

"You can speak in front of the girls," she told him. "They are as aware as I am of the situation here at the school these days."

The police officer drew himself erect. "We just surprised a man loitering around the school. We approached him to question him, and he turned and ran. We gave chase, but he ran up an alley, went between two buildings, and escaped."

Miss Duncan tried to keep from showing her concern but was unable to do so. "Thank you."

"My partner is radioing for more help. I wanted to acquaint you with the situation so you and the girls will use the utmost caution and keep off the street tonight after dark."

"Thank you." Miss Duncan flashed the proper Wellington smile. It was friendly but reserved, not the sort of smile that would give anyone ideas he could get better acquainted, in case he wanted to. It was a politely squelching sort of smile that all Wellington girls were supposed to use with young men they had not been properly introduced to.

When the officer was gone, Miss Duncan turned to the girls with a hoarse whisper. "I was hopeful the man who tried to break into your room, Miss Valdez, had long since gone, but apparently he has not."

Joan's eyes widened fearfully. "Do you think he's the same one?"

"It would be a logical assumption," Miss Duncan retorted. Then, seeing the fear mounting in Emma's eyes, she hedged a little. "At least, we must act as though it is. That's the only way for us to be sure of avoiding trouble."

Felicia had not been taking part in the conversation,

but now she spoke guardedly. "I just wonder if it would be wise to leave the school tonight."

The others stared at her.

"What do you mean?" asked the dean.

"I was just thinking that if we were to leave tonight, we would have a better chance of getting away from whoever is keeping such a close watch on the school."

Miss Duncan thought about that. "That is a good idea, but don't you think it would be better to wait until the very early hours of the morning? There would be less chance than ever of being followed then."

Before dark, Miss Duncan moved Joan's red convertible to a parking place a few paces from the service entrance. To do so, she had to place it in an area of the parking lot reserved for the faculty.

"If anyone asks you why your car is parked there," Miss Duncan told her, "tell them I put it there and to come to me if they have any further questions. That will take care of the matter."

In spite of herself, Joan snickered.

"And just exactly what do you mean by that?" the dean of women wanted to know.

The girl's cheeks crimsoned. "I–I was just thinking the same thing. That certainly would stop their questions."

Miss Duncan eyed her stiffly. "I'm not sure whether I approve of that remark or not."

Without saying anything to anyone else, the three

girls packed their bags and set an alarm for three thirty in the morning.

"I guess we're all set," Joan said finally.

But Felicia was not so sure. "We can't set an alarm so early. At that hour, we'll have the whole floor awake."

"We can't take a chance on oversleeping," Joan countered. "If we do, and Miss Duncan has to wait on us, she'll skin all three of us alive."

"I know," Emma broke in. "We put the alarm under a pillow."

* * *

They got up the following morning at three thirty, dressed, and tiptoed down the back stairs to the service entrance.

Miss Duncan already was waiting for them. She glanced at her watch, frowning severely. "You are seven minutes late," she informed them crisply.

Joan and Miss Duncan went for the car and brought it close to the building so Emma could slip out and into it without being seen. As they pulled out of the school campus, a car approached slowly.

"Scoot down, Miss Valdez," the dean of women ordered. "Quickly."

Emma did as she was told.

Felicia squirmed uncomfortably. It was strange that they would meet a car so near the school at this hour. There was seldom any traffic around Wellington School for Girls after midnight. She turned in her seat and stared after the car as they passed it. Apparently, the two men were not interested in them. At least, they gave no indication that they were.

At the next corner, Miss Duncan had Joan turn right. "Shut off your lights and pull up in front of that parked car. Stop, but don't turn off your engine."

The driver did as she was told. And not a moment too soon. The convertible had scarcely stopped moving when the same car they met moments before went by in the opposite direction. At the intersection, the car came almost to a stop before darting on to the next street.

"That was them!" Felicia cried. "They're looking for us!"

Emma gasped. "You think they find us, no?"

"No, they aren't going to find us," Miss Duncan retorted. "Turn left at the next corner, Miss Bailey. We will go out of town as though we're heading for New York City."

Joan drove in the direction of the turnpike at a moderate rate of speed. Once or twice, they met cars that gave them all a start, thinking the men who had been searching for them had found them. But that did not prove to be the case. The youthful driver went south to the first exit, left the divided highway, and began to make her way northwest over narrow country roads.

"We've lost them," Joan said, sighing her relief.

But Emma was not so sure. She twisted uneasily in the seat beside Felicia and looked back every now and then. "They no quit looking for us so easy. Maybe they find us."

"We're just too smart for them," Joan chirped. "That's all. They're probably driving around the school yet, wondering what happened to us, when the simple truth is that we outfoxed them."

"A Wellington girl is resourceful and ingenious," Miss Duncan reminded her gently, "without being a braggart."

Joan winced.

The first resort on the list was Ed's Alpine Ski Lodge a few miles into New Hampshire. There had been nothing in the description of it in the directory to indicate that it was new, but it was. Sparkling new.

Joan Bailey thought aloud. "There's no use in stopping here. Look at this. It isn't six months old."

The next place on the list was a small lodge operated by a man and his wife. It was a small place with room for less than a dozen guests and had a well-worn, almost run-down look. But the man and his wife were so friendly the girls and Miss Duncan were somewhat reluctant to leave.

"This place is intriguing," the dean of women said as they pulled away. "I would like to come back here sometime and spend a week."

The next place had dropped the name Alpine, they learned.

"We've just taken it over," the new owner boasted. "We changed the name so people would know right away that it's under new management. It used to be just a cheap ski shack, but now it's a high-class ski lodge and winter holiday retreat."

Felicia asked if they had any lockers on the premises.

"Lockers?" His forehead crinkled thoughtfully. "Why would anyone want lockers at a ski lodge?"

"Some resorts have them."

"Well, not places like I operate." He seemed indignant at the suggestion.

His attitude bothered Felicia. "Why would he get so shaken up over such an innocent little question? It was almost as though he was trying to persuade us that he doesn't have lockers." Miss Duncan started for the car.

"Well, where's the next place?" Joan asked.

"It's quite a way," Felicia told her. "I don't think we can make it by dinnertime."

The dean of women paused, her hand on the convertible door. "Well, what are you suggesting? That we spend the night here?"

"I hadn't thought of that," Felicia said.

"Neither had I," Joan broke in, "until right now. I'd sort of like to snoop around here a little while and try to find out if there is anything fishy going on here."

"That," Miss Duncan agreed, "sounds like a great idea."

When the girls went back inside, the man they had talked with previously was not there, and an elderly, graying individual was at the desk.

"Sorry," he said, "but I don't have a bit of space for you. We're booked solid."

Emma's eyes revealed her disappointment.

"I'm right sorry, young lady, but there's nothing I can do about it. We got a whole big party of folks comin' in tonight. A busload of 'em."

"Can you tell us anywhere else that we might go?" Miss Duncan asked.

He thought for a moment. "I tell you what I might do. I just might put you up in the old building if you don't mind a bit of inconvenience."

"I'm sure it will be quite satisfactory."

"It's nice enough for anybody," he went on. "Plenty nice enough for anybody."

The clerk had a bellboy take their things to a pair of rooms on the second floor of a big, rambling wooden structure some distance away from the new building. Once they were alone, the three girls converged on Miss Duncan.

"What are we going to do now?" Felicia wanted to know.

"We find out if number 51 locker is here, no?" Emma asked.

"I thought maybe the three of you could look around while I tend to some other matters."

"Like what?" Joan put in curiously.

"Calling the school to see how things are going, for one thing. And maybe calling some of the ski lodges on your list that are more difficult to get to, for another."

Miss Duncan sat down at the desk and reached for the phone.

"We go now?" Emma asked eagerly.

"I suppose it's not going to be any worse now than later," Joan retorted. "If we've got to do it, we'd just as well get it over with. But I can tell you one thing. The manager's not going to like it if he catches us snooping around."

"What makes you think he's going to catch us?" Felicia asked.

The girls crept out into the shadowy hallway and looked in one direction and then the other fearfully. There may have been other guests in their end of the big building, but they didn't see anybody. The naked bulbs suspended from the ceiling at widely spaced intervals glowed so feebly it seemed to Felicia that they were more to light the premises against intruders than for guests. She slid her feet noiselessly across the threadbare carpet and reached out her hand to steady herself against the pale wall.

"I don't know about you," Joan muttered, "but this place gives me the creeps."

Felicia did not reply. She didn't dare to voice her own growing uneasiness.

"This is a waste of time," Joan continued. "I think we'd just as well go back."

"No!" Emma whispered. "We have to find number 51 locker."

They reached the stairs and were just starting down stealthily, when the outside door on the main floor below them opened and the ski lodge manager burst in.

"Oh!" Joan gasped when she saw him.

"I'm sorry. I didn't mean to startle you." He gave them a broad, toothy grin that did nothing to allay their uneasiness. "I am Mr. Rivers, the manager. I came over to apologize for having given you rooms over here. I can't understand Mr. Bloom doing a thing like that."

"It is sort of scary here," Joan admitted.

"I can well understand why. We scarcely ever use this old building, except for overflow crowds. We have other rooms for you."

"You don't have to do that," Felicia said quickly. "The accommodations we have are all right for one night. In fact, we're quite comfortable."

Her roommate withered her with a look.

"But I insist." He came up the stairs. "And I'm sure your Miss Duncan will agree with me."

Miss Duncan did agree with him. He phoned for

a bellboy and moved the foursome into beautiful adjoining rooms in a choice part of the main lodge.

"I don't get this," Felicia said. "First, we are told that they are all booked up. Then we are given rooms like these. It seems fishy to me."

"Don't knock it," Joan exclaimed. "I'm beginning to like this place better all the time."

Felicia sat down at the desk, that vague uneasiness continuing to build within her. She couldn't define it or explain it, but it was there, nevertheless.

"Why would the lodge manager insist that we take rooms over here?"

"His conscience got to bothering him over having us in rooms like the other guy put us in."

"I can't buy that. Especially when you think about the way he treated us when we first came. He acted as though he didn't want us to stay at all. Now he gives us the best rooms in the house almost."

"I think same thing, maybe," Emma put in. "Like he want to get us out of old building, no?"

Miss Duncan, who had not taken part in the conversation until that moment, spoke up. "I have the same impression, especially in the light of what happened when I made my phone calls."

The girls stared at her.

"What happened?" Joan asked fearfully.

"I wasn't going to tell you, but now I feel that you have a right to know." She paused momentarily.

"Somebody was listening in while I called the school and two other lodges."

There was a short silence.

"That means," Miss Duncan continued, "that somebody here knows where we're from and could have a good idea as to what we're doing."

Felicia's cheeks went ashen, and her blue eyes were round and staring. This was not what she had expected at all. "But why would anyone listen in on your calls?"

"That's something I can't figure out, unless–" Her voice caught.

"Unless what?"

"Unless someone here was suspicious when we asked about lockers and wanted to find out more about our purpose for being here."

All was still as they thought about that briefly.

"Do you suppose it could have anything to do with our being moved out of the old building over to here?" Joan whispered, breaking the stillness.

"It could be," Miss Duncan said quietly, "if the old building should contain some lockers that somebody didn't want us to stumble onto."

Emma's eyes gleamed. "You think the number 51 locker is in the old building, no?"

"I suppose it could be." The dean of women leaned forward and spoke as softly as though the corners of the room had ears. "But that is something we've got to find out!"

CHAPTER 9

UNEXPECTED COOPERATION

The girls went down to dinner, taking a table near the window. Although most of the guests were talking enthusiastically about the condition of the snow and skiing, the girls and their older companion were much more serious. They leaned forward until their four heads almost touched in the center of the table and spoke in low tones.

"We've got to get back to that old building and give it a good combing," Felicia said.

"But how are we going to do that?" Joan asked guardedly. "They're keeping a close watch on us, you can be sure of that."

Miss Duncan turned in her chair to survey the lobby of the lodge. "I just realized something. Do you know that the rooms we are staying in now can only be reached by the front stairs?"

"Oh?" Joan queried. "What is so significant about that?"

"So, we cannot leave our rooms or go up to them without being seen by the clerk on duty. Without making any special effort, they can watch us all the time."

"Very clever," Felicia murmured.

"And scary," Joan added. "I don't know about you, but I don't much like the idea of being watched all the time."

"What that mean?" Emma asked, her concern growing. "Won't we get to find out if Uncle Hermano had been here?"

Before anyone could answer her, the manager, Mr. Rivers, came mincing up to their table. He asked if the rooms were satisfactory and if the service and food suited them.

"Everything has been very nice," Miss Duncan answered.

"I am so glad. If you are pleased, perhaps more young ladies from Wellington School for Girls will want to come here skiing."

At the mention of the name of the school, four heads snapped up.

"How did you know we are from Wellington?" Joan blurted.

Now it was the manager's turn to be flustered.

"I–" Sweat pearled his high forehead. "You signed the name of the school on the register."

"I beg your pardon," Miss Duncan retorted icily, "but I did not write the name of the school on the register. We at Wellington are most jealous of our name. We only permit it to be used when groups are out on regularly scheduled school functions."

By this time, Mr. Rivers had gained control of himself once more. "I was just kidding. Actually, I recognized you when you came in, Miss Duncan. You see, I used to go with a girl who went to Wellington a number of years ago, and I became well acquainted with you by reputation."

Miss Duncan was unimpressed. "I see," she retorted coldly.

The manager's manner changed once more. He was confident and self-assured. "When you have finished dinner, would you mind stopping in at my office for a moment?" His voice lowered. "I think I can help you."

For a moment or two, the girls ate in silence.

"He act nice this time," Emma said.

"He lied," Miss Duncan answered curtly. "And one can never trust a person who lies."

"You think he found out about our being from Wellington by listening in on your telephone conversation?" Felicia asked.

"Exactly. It is the only way he could know."

When they finished eating and left the dining hall, the manager was standing in the lobby waiting for them.

"I was afraid you would go on up to your rooms," he said frankly, "and I didn't want to miss you."

He ushered them into his large office and closed the door carefully.

"Now," Miss Duncan said, facing him. "What do you want to talk to us about that's so secretive you have to bring us in here and close the door?"

His smile was fleeting. "You don't trust anyone, do you?"

"Quite the contrary," the dean of women informed him. "I always trust those who are found worthy of trust."

He flinched. "I'm going to forget you said that."

Miss Duncan acted as though she had not even heard him. "What is it you want to talk with us about?" she repeated.

The manager leaned against his desk. "I knew Hermano Valdez," he began. "In fact, he used to work for me."

Emma's eyes lighted. "You knew my uncle?"

"You must be Emma." His smile flashed. "He talked about you a great deal, Emma. He said that you were his favorite and most beautiful niece."

"Gracias."

"When we built the new building, we did not put in lockers for skis and gear, but we didn't remove them from the old lodge. Some of the helpers used those that were not reserved for the guests. That was how Hermano came to have a locker here."

"Number 51?" Emma asked incredulously.

"Number 51."

The girl gasped.

"Why didn't you tell us this before?" Miss Duncan wanted to know.

"I wasn't sure just why you were inquiring about lockers. That's all."

"And something happened to cause you to change your mind?" the dean of women persisted.

"No." He shook his head. "I just got to thinking it over. I decided that if Miss Duncan, the dean at such a prominent school for girls, was involved in it, it would have to be all right."

In spite of herself, Miss Duncan beamed. That was the ideal they worked toward at Wellington – a flawless reputation for each student.

"Now, if you will come with me," the manager concluded, "I'll take you out and show you the locker." He opened a drawer and removed a master key.

"We have the key," Emma exclaimed, holding it up.

That seemed to surprise Mr. Rivers. His lips parted as though to question her about the key, but instead he clamped them shut tightly and thrust the key into his pocket. "Oh, well, no matter. I'll take my key along, too, in case we need it."

He led them down the front steps, along the walk to the edge of the lodge, and turned in the direction of the older building. "I hope you will find what you're looking for."

Miss Duncan scowled her disapproval at the questioning tone in his voice, but she did not respond to it.

The lockers were on the main floor of the aging wooden structure and well to the back. The corridor the manager headed for was dark and forbidding.

"We don't use this part of the structure anymore," he said, "so the lighting, among other things, is in a state of disrepair."

He took a flashlight from his pocket and switched it on. The faint yellow beam revealed a carpet so covered with dust the design was scarcely legible. Cobwebs angled across door openings, and a faint, musty odor pinched their nostrils.

"I probably should have waited until morning to bring you here, but I am anxious that you know we have nothing to hide. I–" His voice caught in a sudden spasm of his throat.

There before them a locker door sagged open on its rusty hinges. At first, the girls and Miss Duncan could scarcely believe it. They stared numbly.

Emma gasped aloud. "Number 51 locker!" Her taut voice broke.

Felicia extended a trembling finger and traced the figures in the metal. There was no mistaking it. It was locker 51.

"I can't understand it!" Mr. Rivers exclaimed numbly. "It was all right this afternoon when I was out here. But it's not now!"

"That is quite obvious!" Miss Duncan exclaimed.

The girls eyed one another, making no effort to hide their consternation.

"Somebody break into Uncle Hermano's locker!" Emma managed weakly. "And what was in it is stolen, no?"

The agitated ski lodge manager apologized profusely, assuring them that he would not stop until the individuals who were responsible for breaking into the locker were caught and justly punished.

"It is regrettable," he muttered. "Most regrettable."

"Unfortunately," Miss Duncan said, her voice stern, "recognizing that this theft is regrettable isn't going to help Miss Valdez get money enough to stay at Wellington."

Miss Duncan's terse statement stopped the manager suddenly, as though he had been caught by the foot and held motionless.

"No," he said, staring at Emma. "No, it won't help her, and that's a pity."

Miss Duncan insisted that the girls go back to their rooms immediately.

"But–" Joan started to protest.

"We must get to bed at once," she said. "Tomorrow will be another hard day."

The lodge manager squinted at her. "You'll go back to town in the morning, eh?" he asked hopefully.

"I'm not sure what we'll do," the dean of women retorted. "We haven't made up our minds."

In their room some minutes later, Emma burst

into tears. "It is no use. I no can get money. I have to leave school."

Miss Duncan put a hand on her shoulder clumsily and looked sadly at Felicia who knew well enough what Miss Duncan's eyes were saying. The dean wanted to help Emma, but she couldn't arouse false hope. There was no money for a scholarship for her and no prospect for getting any. The girl would have to leave school. Felicia knew that the dean of women wanted desperately to be able to comfort Emma, but she had to be honest too.

"I'm going to my room," Miss Duncan said. "If you need me, just call."

With that, the three girls were alone. For a time, they looked at each other in silence.

"What will you do if you have to leave Wellington, Emma?" Joan wanted to know.

The Cuban girl shook her head. By this time, she had managed to stop crying. "I not know," she said, lapsing into silence once more.

"We'd better have our Bible reading and go to bed," Felicia put in. "There's no knowing what time Miss Duncan will insist on getting us up."

She opened the Bible to the book and chapter where she and Joan were reading. She was about to begin when Emma broke in.

"You remember when you talk to me about the claim Jesus Christ have on my life, no?"

Felicia nodded. "I remember. Why?" She spoke the word prayerfully, hopefully.

"You say He give me strength and courage I need?"

"That's right. Being a Christian is a life to be lived, and Christ helps us to live as we should."

Emma seemed determined to get the matter straight in her own mind.

"You mean He would help me even if I–I have to leave Wellington?"

"Even if you have to leave Wellington," Felicia told her. "It doesn't matter where you go or what happens to you. Jesus will be there giving you the strength you need to live for Him."

Emma thought about that. "If I live for Him, will He help me to–to stay in school?" she asked at last.

Felicia hesitated. "Maybe He will and maybe not. Christ doesn't promise to work everything out just the way we want it. What He does promise is to help us take the trials that come our way."

Starting at the beginning, Felicia explained how God had given people the law, but we couldn't keep it, so God sent Jesus Christ to live a perfect, sinless life, die on the cross and rise again, so we can now confess our sin and put our trust in Him for salvation."

"I believe in God," Emma said weakly.

"That's a good start," Felicia told her, "but the Bible says that we have to confess our sin and put our trust in Christ. We have to have a personal relationship with Him if we are to go to heaven. We have to meet

His conditions before we can be saved. And Jesus tells us in the Bible, *I am the way, the truth and the life: no man comes to the Father, except by me.*"

Emma tried to speak, but her lower lip trembled so that she could not. It was several minutes before she could say anything.

"I–I have no one in America," she whispered. "I am so tired of being alone – of having to figure out everything myself."

"The Bible says that Christ will not leave or forsake us," Felicia reminded her quietly.

That did it. Emma knelt beside the bed in the ski lodge room she shared with Joan and Felicia and gave her heart and her life to Jesus Christ. The other two girls knelt beside her, thanking God silently for this decision of Emma's. It made everything that had happened worthwhile.

* * *

Felicia had supposed that Miss Duncan would rout them out before dawn the following morning, but such was not the case. The dean was up early enough herself. Felicia heard her moving around the room. But when she knocked on the door and looked in, Miss Duncan was at the desk writing emails. She gave every indication of being there for some time.

In the other room, Joan took the news gleefully. "I'm going to get me another hour's sleep."

"And I write home to my grandfather to tell him what happen to me last night," Emma put in. "I not know if I can explain to him how this giving Christ control change my life, but–" Words failed her.

"Well," Felicia said, "I'm going for a walk."

Joan opened one eye. "If you find any cute boys, come and tell me."

"You'll have to find your own," Felicia retorted, laughing.

She left the ski lodge and walked briskly along the snow-packed path. It was early, and most of the guests were just getting up or having breakfast. Few were out on the slopes yet.

Felicia was at the corner of the old frame building when she was surprised to see the manager come out of the side door and glance furtively about, as though wanting to avoid being seen. As their eyes met, he started uneasily.

"Oh, hello, Mr. Rivers." Felicia managed a smile.

"I didn't expect to see you out so early," he said.

"You never know where you'll see me," she told him impishly, "or what I'll be doing."

That seemed to disturb him even more. He took a step or two toward the back of the building uncertainly and stopped as though he had just made up his mind to put off doing something that was most important.

"Well," he said, "it is a beautiful morning."

Reluctantly, or so it seemed to Felicia, he turned and went back inside.

For an instant or two, she remained motionless. The man did seem to have an errand that he didn't want her to know anything about. She wasn't sure why she did it, except that his actions were so suspicious, but she made her way to the rear of the building and looked around curiously.

It was, indeed, a very old building. Some of the windowpanes at the back were cracked, and a few odd pieces of junk were propped up against the weathered siding to rust into uselessness. There were two old iron bedsteads, a wrought-iron lamp, and a couple of car wheels of long-forgotten origin.

And then Felicia saw it – a lady's ski boot half buried in the snow. At first, she eyed it quizzically, wondering why a single ski boot would have been thrown away. It did look strangely familiar, but she could not remember where she had seen it.

Almost mechanically, Felicia went over and picked it up. Closer examination proved even more perplexing. The sole had been ripped half away, the heel had been torn off, and the counter in the back had been cut free at the top to expose anything that might have been hidden behind it.

She turned it thoughtfully in her hand, trying to recall whether she had ever seen it before or not. Then suddenly she remembered. This ski boot was the same as the one Emma had hanging on her wall back at school! It must have been in Uncle Hermano's locker! That was the only explanation.

She was still standing there holding it when a footstep sounded at the corner of the building. She spun around to see the ski lodge manager staring at her! A faint, haunting grin did little to soften the anger of his eyes.

"Looking for something?" he asked pointedly.

"Not now." Tightening her grip on the ski boot, she pushed past him.

"One of our guests threw it away," he said, indicating the boot with a jerk of his head.

"I can't imagine why!" Felicia's heart was pounding a savage beat as she hurried around the corner of the old building.

CHAPTER 10

GRANDFATHER'S PROVISION

Felicia scurried over the frozen path, half expecting a powerful hand to clamp on her shoulder at any instant and tear the mutilated ski boot from her grasp. But it did not happen, and, in a moment, she was inside the lodge.

By this time, the lobby was filling with early rising skiers. They looked curiously at the torn ski boot Felicia carried. She felt her cheeks tinge with crimson as she hurried up the stairs to their room.

Joan sat up as Felicia burst through the door. "You're back early. I thought you'd walk for an hour." Her gaze fixed on the ski boot Felicia held in her hand. "Where did you get that?"

Emma, who was still writing to her grandfather, looked up. She gasped audibly when she saw the ski boot. "Mama's ski boot! Where you get him?"

"Out behind the old building," Felicia explained. "It must have been in your uncle's locker."

Emma took the boot tenderly, turning it in her hands as though it was some sort of a precious jewel. "Why they do *this* to him?"

Felicia studied the boot with care. "It looks to me as though they were looking for something they thought was hidden in it."

Joan nodded. "That's the way it looks to me too."

Emma could not hide her concern. "You think maybe they find?" she asked fearfully. "No?"

Joan went over the boot that had been almost ripped to pieces, studying it intently.

"You know, I don't think they found what they were looking for in this boot," she said at last. "There's no hole in the heel or underneath the sole where anything could have been hidden. And the counter fits too snug to have concealed anything."

Felicia nodded. "I'm sure you're right. There's no evidence that would indicate anything was ever hidden in *this* boot."

The inflection in her voice caused Emma to jerk erect. "Why you say it that way? What do you mean?"

Felicia didn't know what her Cuban friend was talking about.

"Why you say nothing was hidden in *this* boot?" Emma repeated. "You think maybe something is hidden in the one I have at school?"

Felicia and Joan stared at one another.

"I'd never thought of that," the Cartright girl exclaimed. "But it just could be!"

It was too much for Emma to grasp. She looked from one girl to the other and then back at the ripped-apart ski boot. "It couldn't be. If it had been, my grandfather, he would have tell me. He no let me run out of money and have to leave school, maybe."

That did present a problem, the girls had to admit. It didn't seem likely that her grandfather would have let her take the ski boot with something valuable in it unless he hinted at that fact.

"How did it come that you brought the ski boot with you when you left Cuba?" Felicia asked. "Was it your idea or your grandfather's?"

Emma paused, thinking back to that dark night when she had boarded the boat for the dangerous journey to Florida.

"My mother die when I am little," she explained. "I have nothing of hers except her ski boots. I want to bring both of them with me, but my grandfather, he insist I only take one."

Felicia frowned. "That's strange."

"He say something about the boat have such a big load, but I think it something else, like maybe he want to keep one boot for himself. He have nothing of hers to remember her by either."

"Then how did Uncle Hermano get this one?" Joan asked.

Emma shrugged expressively. "Who knows?"

"Did your grandfather say anything that would make you think there might be something hidden in the boot you had?" Felicia asked.

She shook her head. "He say nothing about it except only that I could just take one of them."

Joan and Felicia thought about that. It scarcely seemed possible that Emma's grandfather would have let her take a boot with money or jewels hidden in it and not give her at least one small clue as to what she was carrying.

"But," Joan said, "I suppose it's entirely possible, even though we can't figure out why."

They were still discussing the matter when Miss Duncan knocked on their door and came in. She picked up the ski boot by its heavy lace and looked at it.

"It seems to me that I've seen another ski boot like this one somewhere," she said, "only it hadn't been treated quite so roughly."

"Sí," Emma answered. With the help of the other two girls, she told Miss Duncan the entire story of the ski boots, including the theory Felicia and Joan had developed.

"It sounds logical," the dean of women admitted, "but the most logical events aren't always the truth."

Still holding the boot by the long metal shoelace end, she gave it back to Emma.

"I am glad to get this one back," the girl said sadly, "but I don't know if I ever find anyone to put it together or not." She looked at it, her dark eyes somber.

"Why don't you put the ski boot away now, Miss Valdez?" Miss Duncan suggested gently. "It's past time for us to have breakfast."

Emma would have left the boot on the floor beside her bed, but Felicia suggested that she hide it in a less conspicuous spot.

"I don't know whether it means anything or not," Felicia said, uneasiness creeping into her voice, "but the lodge manager saw me pick up the ski boot a little while ago."

"Let me have it," Miss Duncan said crisply. "I'll hide it so it can't be found."

She came back from her room moments later. "Now," she announced decisively, "let's go to breakfast."

They were sitting in the dining room waiting to be served when the cashier approached their table.

"Pardon me," she said, "but are you Miss Duncan?"

"That's right."

"I have a call for you."

The girls waited breathlessly for the dean to return. When she came back several minutes later, it was clearly evident that there was something wrong. Her cheeks were pale, and the lights in her eyes had gone out. The three students eyed her questioningly but dared not give voice to their concern. Not with Miss Duncan. Instead, they waited until she had sat down and sipped her coffee. At last, she directed her attention to Emma.

"I am afraid I have some bad news for you, my dear," she began.

"Bad news?" The girl's dark eyes were round and staring. "What is this bad news?"

"Your room in the dorm was broken into last night," the dean of women continued.

"Was anything taken?" Emma asked woodenly.

"Only the ski boot you had hanging on the wall."

The attractive young Cuban señorita gasped audibly.

"It was found behind a clump of bushes on the edge of the campus this morning," Miss Duncan continued. "It had been torn apart in the same way the boot upstairs had been ripped up."

The corners of Felicia's lips tightened.

"Did it look as though they found anything in it?" Joan wanted to know.

"That is the strange part," Miss Duncan said. "The police examined the ski boot carefully but could find no evidence that anything had ever been hidden in it!"

Felicia sucked in her breath sharply. Her companions stared at her.

"Now, what's the matter with you?" Joan demanded.

"Don't you see?" she whispered, her excitement growing. "If the thieves and the police both went over the ski boot that was stolen from Emma's room, the chances are there was nothing in it. The police would send it to their laboratory and x-ray it or something."

"I'm sure you're right," the dean of women said, "but I can't understand why that's anything to get so excited about."

"Maybe it isn't," Felicia said, "but maybe it is." She leaned closer to be sure she wasn't overheard. "We ought to go over the ski boot we've got upstairs. It could be that the thieves missed something."

"It doesn't look like it to me," Miss Duncan replied. "I don't see where anything could be hidden in that boot and be overlooked."

Emma, too, had lost heart. She was sure now that nothing was going to be found to help her. "It is no use for to look anymore. I have to quit school."

Felicia saw the tears in her eyes. "You can give up if you want to, but I'm not giving up yet."

Felicia wanted to leave immediately and go back to their rooms, but Miss Duncan insisted they finish breakfast first.

"We may have a long, hard day ahead of us," she informed them.

Felicia was so excited she scarcely realized what she was eating. She was the first through and had to wait what seemed to be ages for Miss Duncan and the others to finish breakfast.

"Don't act so excited, Felicia," Joan whispered. "Be calm. Be nonchalant like a proper Wellington girl ought to be."

Felicia glared at her friend. "You can make fun of

me if you want to, but I still think there's something in that boot that nobody's found yet."

"And you're going to find it, I suppose."

Felicia frowned. "Just wait," she murmured quietly. "Just you wait until we get upstairs and go over that boot again."

Miss Duncan went directly to her room and returned with the boot. "Here it is," she said, making no attempt to hide her own low opinion of Felicia's guess. "But how anything could be hidden in here and not have been found already, I'll never know."

Felicia took the ski boot and began to look it over carefully. What Miss Duncan and Joan said certainly appeared to be true. Every place in the ski boot where it seemed that anything could have been hidden had been ripped open. There wasn't another hiding place.

"You'd just as well give up," Joan scoffed. "You're not going to find anything in there."

"I'm not ready to quit yet," she retorted doggedly. She turned the boot once more thoughtfully.

Then she noticed the metal ends on the lace. They didn't look large enough to hold anything, but–

"Joan, have you got a fingernail file?"

"Right here. Why?"

"Let me have it for a minute."

"Don't tell me you've found something!"

"I don't know for sure."

Using the file, she pried one of the metal ends

open. "There's nothing in there," she said, more to herself than to her companion.

"What did you expect to find? A trunkful of silver dollars?"

Felicia went to work on the other one. It was even harder to open than the first had been. A couple of times she was about to give up. But at last, she succeeded in prying the metal apart. There *was* an object inside. A tiny roll of something!

"Look!" Felicia cried.

Her companions crowded close to her.

"What is it?" Emma asked, her voice stretched taut.

"I don't know," Felicia told her, "but it certainly isn't something that belongs in a bootlace."

Miss Duncan was visibly shaken. "I know what it is," she whispered tensely. "It's microfilm!"

The girls stared at her, disappointment gleaming in their eyes.

"How's that going to help Emma stay in Wellington?" Joan asked.

"I don't know. It depends on what's on it."

Felicia remembered what Emma had said about her grandfather wanting to do something to help the United States. "Maybe this is it," she said, half to herself.

Miss Duncan had gotten to her feet slowly. "Our job now is to get away from here without arousing suspicion."

"Do you think there's somebody here who might try to stop us?" Joan whispered, suddenly growing numb.

Miss Duncan did not answer her directly. "There is someone who is going to great lengths to get this microfilm. We can't take any chances."

They were all silent for a time.

"I have it," the dean of women said at last. "Put that metal end back in place, Felicia, and you two get your bags packed."

Felicia eyed her curiously. "What are we going to do?"

"We're going to leave a little smoke screen," Miss Duncan said. "We're going to make them think we didn't find anything in the old ski boot either."

"But how?"

"You wait and see."

Moments later, she called for a bellboy to carry their bags down to the car.

"You sure didn't stay long," he said curiously, looking over the room.

"No, we didn't," Miss Duncan answered cryptically.

"Hey," he said, "you're leaving that old ski boot."

She laughed shortly. "It's quite obvious that it isn't any good."

The manager was nowhere in sight when they left the lodge, but he was watching from the doorway as they pulled away.

"Think we got away with it?" Joan asked uneasily.

"We'll soon know," Felicia said.

They were just pulling out onto the highway when a car backed out of the parking lot and turned around.

"Here he comes," Felicia said under her breath. "You'd better step on it."

Two miles down the road, Miss Duncan ordered Joan to take a sharp left.

"But that's not the way back to school," the girl protested.

"Maybe it isn't, but it's the closest way to a town with a police force."

The car behind them was gaining steadily when Joan swung around a sharp corner off the highway and into the picturesque little mountain village. The other car turned too; but, when Joan stopped beside the police station, they sped away.

"We've made it!" Felicia cried. "We're safe!"

* * *

It was the middle of the next afternoon when Mr. Powers, the police detective, and a tall well-dressed stranger who represented some department of the United States government came out to Wellington School for Girls. Miss Duncan called Felicia and Joan and Emma into her office.

"We have been examining the microfilm," the stranger said, "and have found it most helpful. Your grandfather performed a great service for our country, young lady."

"Sí." Her smile broadened. "He say he help this America he love so much."

"He had microfilmed the pictures and names and other information of twenty-eight enemy agents who are operating in this country, including Rivero, the manager of the ski lodge you stopped at. He's in custody now."

The girls glanced at one another.

"So that's why he was so anxious to find the secret of that boot," Felicia said.

"The film is going to be of great value to our government," the agent said. "I want you to know that." Then he turned to Emma once more. "And it has an item of interest to you too. It contains the numbers of a bank account your grandfather opened for you in Switzerland a number of years ago. With the numbers, you will be able to draw on it as you wish."

She stared incredulously. "You–you mean I won't have to quit school?"

"Not unless you want to."

The Cuban girl beamed. "Thank You, God."

The stranger's eyes widened. "What?"

"I said, 'Thank You, God,'" Emma repeated. "I was thanking Him for making it possible for me to stay here in America."

"Oh." The man seemed embarrassed. "That's what I thought you said."

Felicia and Joan eyed each other, beaming. Everything had worked out wonderfully – better than they had even dared to hope for. And best of all, Emma was now a Christian.

THE
FELICIA CARTRIGHT
SERIES

Felicia Cartright, a petite blonde who is one of the most popular students at Wellington School for Girls, has a surprising inclination toward mysteries. If a mysterious situation arises, it either makes its way to Felicia, or Felicia somehow finds it. Though this is a bit trying for her happy-go-lucky roommate, Joan Bailey, it does prevent life from becoming monotonous. It also enables Bernard Palmer, the popular author of the "Danny Orlis" books, to write an entertaining series of stories for girls aged twelve to eighteen.

The mysteries range from a valuable missing antique to an attempt by claim jumpers to steal a deposit of tungsten ore. There's excitement and action galore—but there's also spiritual guidance and blessing because Felicia and her partner-in-adventure love the Lord and take Him into account in all their experiences.